PENGUIN BOOKS

MY FAIR LADY

Alan Jay Lerner graduated from Harvard in 1940, and having already written two Hasty Pudding shows hoped to work for Broadway theatres. Instead he spent two years writing radio scripts. Then, in collaboration with Frederick Loewe, he wrote in one week a musical, *What's Up* (1943). In 1945 he wrote *The Day Before Spring*, and in 1947, again with Loewe, the successful *Brigadoon*. He then collaborated with Kurt Weill on *Love Life*, and wrote the story and screenplay for the film *An American in Paris*. In 1951 he and Loewe had another success with *Paint Your Wagon*. *My Fair Lady*, based on Shaw's *Pygmalion*, was produced in 1960, as was *Camelot*. He also worked on the film versions of *Gigi*, *Royal Wedding*, and *My Fair Lady*. He died in 1986.

MY FAIR LADY

A musical play in two acts
based on *Pygmalion* by
Bernard Shaw

Adaptation and lyrics by
ALAN JAY LERNER

Music by
FREDERICK LOEWE

PENGUIN BOOKS

PENGUIN BOOKS

Published by the Penguin Group
Penguin Books Ltd, 27 Wrights Lane, London W8 5TZ, England
Penguin Putnam Inc., 375 Hudson Street, New York, New York 10014, USA
Penguin Books Australia Ltd, Ringwood, Victoria, Australia
Penguin Books Canada Ltd, 10 Alcorn Avenue, Toronto, Ontario, Canada M4V 3B2
Penguin Books (NZ) Ltd, 182–190 Wairau Road, Auckland 10, New Zealand

Penguin Books Ltd, Registered Offices: Harmondsworth, Middlesex, England

First published 1956
Published in Great Britain by Max Reinhardt and Constable 1958
Published in Penguin Books 1959
23 25 27 29 30 28 26 24

Printed in England by Clays Ltd, St Ives plc
Set in Monotype Bembo

CONTENTS

NOTE

For the published version of *Pygmalion*, Shaw wrote a preface and an epilogue which he called a sequel. I have omitted the preface because the information contained therein is less pertinent to *My Fair Lady* than it is to *Pygmalion*.

I have omitted the sequel because in it Shaw explains how Eliza ends not with Higgins but with Freddy and – Shaw and Heaven forgive me! – I am not certain he is right.

A. J. L.

MUSICAL SYNOPSIS

ACT ONE

ACT TWO

LIST OF PLATES

We are grateful to Messrs Warner Bros for permission to use the illustrations in this edition, which come from their film production of My Fair Lady

CAST

The stage version of *My Fair Lady* was first presented in England at the Theatre Royal, Drury Lane, on Wednesday, 30 April 1958, with Julie Andrews as Eliza Doolittle, Rex Harrison as Henry Higgins, and Stanley Holloway as Alfred Doolittle.

Cast of the film version:

Eliza	*Audrey Hepburn*
Professor Higgins	*Rex Harrison*
Alfred Doolittle	*Stanley Holloway*
Colonel Pickering	*Wilfrid Hyde White*
Mrs Higgins	*Gladys Cooper*
Freddie	*Jeremy Brett*
Zoltan Karpathy	*Theodore Bikel*
Mrs Pearce	*Mona Washbourne*
Mrs Eynsford-Hill	*Isobel Elsom*
Butler	*John Holland*

✳✳✳✳✳✳✳✳✳✳✳✳

ACT ONE

✳✳✳✳✳✳✳✳✳✳✳✳

SCENE ONE

Outside the Royal Opera House, Covent Garden. Time: After-theatre, a cold March night.

At rise of curtain: The opera is just over. Richly gowned, beautifully tailored Londoners are pouring from the Opera House and making their way across Covent Garden in search of taxis. Some huddle together under the columns of St Paul's Church which are partially in view on one side of the stage. On the opposite side, there is a smudge-pot fire around which a quartet of costermongers are warming themselves. Calls of 'Taxi' punctuate the icy air.

THREE STREET ENTERTAINERS, BUSKERS, rush on to perform a few acrobatic tricks, stunts, and dance steps. They detain the crowd for a moment. The female member of the trio passes the hat as her two associates continue and reach the 'climax' of their act.

MRS EYNSFORD-HILL, a middle-aged lady in evening dress, and her son FREDDY, a young man of twenty, also in evening dress, come through the crowd in search of a taxi. One of the buskers collides into him. He is thrown backwards and strikes a figure hidden behind a group of people who now comes flying forward and lands in a heap. She is a flower girl, ELIZA DOOLITTLE. Her basket of flowers has been knocked from her hands and her violets scattered about. She is not at all an attractive person. She is perhaps eighteen, perhaps twenty, hardly older. She wears a little sailor hat of black straw that has long been exposed to the dust and soot of London and has seldom if ever been brushed. Her hair needs washing rather badly; its mousy colour can hardly be natural. She wears a shoddy shawl, a dirty blouse with a coarse apron. Her boots are much the worse for wear. She is no doubt as clean as she can afford to be; but compared to the ladies she is very dirty. Her features are no worse than theirs; but their condition leaves something to be desired, and she needs the services of a dentist.

ELIZA: Aaaooowww!

FREDDY [*clumsily trying to help her*]: I'm frightfully sorry.

ELIZA [*wailing*]: Two bunches of violets trod in the mud! A full day's wages. Why don't you look where you're going?

MRS EYNSFORD-HILL: Get a taxi, Freddy. Do you want me to catch pneumonia?

FREDDY: I'm sorry, Mother. I'll get a taxi right away. [*To* ELIZA] Sorry. [*He goes.*]

[COLONEL PICKERING *emerges dressed in evening clothes and looking for a taxi. He is a middle-aged gentleman of the amiable military type.*]

ELIZA [*to* MRS EYNSFORD-HILL]: Oh, he's your son, is he? Well, if you'd done your duty by him as a mother should, you wouldn't let him spoil a poor girl's flowers and then run away without paying.

MRS EYNSFORD-HILL: Go on about your business, my girl. [*She follows her son.*]

ELIZA [*muttering to herself, as she collects her flowers*]: Two bunches of violets trod in the mud.

PICKERING [*calling off*]: Taxi! Taxi!

ELIZA [*to* PICKERING]: I say, Captain, buy a flower off a poor girl.

PICKERING: I'm sorry. I haven't any change.

ELIZA: I can change half a crown. Here, take this for tuppence.

PICKERING [*trying his pockets*]: I really haven't any – stop: here's three ha'pence, if that's any use to you.

ELIZA [*disappointed, but thinking three halfpence better than nothing*]: Thank you, sir.

A BYSTANDER [*to* ELIZA]: Here, you be careful. Better give him a flower fer it. There's a bloke there behind the pillar taking down every blessed word you're saying.

[*The* CROWD *turns to look behind the pillar.*]

ELIZA [*springing up terrified*]: I ain't done nothin' wrong by speakin' to the gentleman! I've a right to sell flowers if I keep off the kerb.

I'm a respectable girl; so help me, I never spoke to him except to ask him to buy a flower off me.

[*There is a general hubbub, mostly sympathetic to* ELIZA, *but deprecating her excessive sensibility*.]

ANOTHER BYSTANDER: What's the row?

A HOXTON MAN: What's all the bloomin' noise?

A SELSEY MAN: There's a tec takin' her down.

ELIZA [*crying wildly – to* PICKERING]: Oh, sir, don't let him charge me! You dunno what it means to me. They'll take away my character and drive me on the streets for speakin' to gentlemen.

[PROFESSOR HIGGINS *pivots around the post and into view*.]

HIGGINS: There! There! There! Who's hurting you, you silly girl! What do you take me for?

ELIZA [*to* HIGGINS – *still hysterical*]: On my Bible oath, I never said a word . . .

HIGGINS [*overbearing, but good-humored*]: Oh, shut up, shut up. Do I look like a policeman?

ELIZA: Then what did you take down my words for? How do I know whether you took me down right? You just show me what you wrote about me.

[HIGGINS *opens his book and holds it steadily under her nose, though the pressure of the mob trying to read it over his shoulders would upset a weaker man*.]

What's this? That ain't proper writing. I can't read that.

HIGGINS: I can. [*Reads, reproducing her pronunciation*] I say, Captain, buy a flower off a poor girl.

ELIZA: It's because I called him Captain! I meant no harm. [*To* PICKERING] Oh, sir, don't let him lay a charge agen me for a word like that. You . . .

PICKERING: Charge! I make no charge. [*To* HIGGINS] Really, sir, if you are a detective, you need not begin protecting me against molestation by young women until I ask you. Anybody could see the girl meant no harm.

THE SELSEY MAN: He ain't a tec. He's a gentleman. Look at his shoes.

HIGGINS [*turning on him genially*]: And how are all your people down at Selsey?

THE SELSEY MAN [*suspiciously*]: Who told you my people come from Selsey?

HIGGINS: Never mind. They did. [*To* ELIZA] How do you come to be up so far east? You were born in Lisson Grove.

ELIZA [*appalled*]: Oooooh, what harm is there in my leaving Lisson Grove? It wasn't fit for a pig to live in; and I had to pay four-and-six a week. Oh, boo-hoo-oo –

HIGGINS: Live where you like; but stop that noise. [*With pad in hand, he becomes interested in the accents of the men grouped around the fire.*]

PICKERING [*to* ELIZA]: Come, come! He can't touch you; you have a right to live where you please.

ELIZA [*subsiding into a brooding melancholy and talking very low-spiritedly to herself*]: I'm a good girl, I am.

THE HOXTON MAN: Do you know where *I* come from?

HIGGINS [*promptly*]: Hoxton.

THE HOXTON MAN [*amazed*]: Well, who said I didn't! Blimey, you know everything, you do.

[*Titterings. Popular interest in the note-taker's performance increases.*]

ANOTHER BYSTANDER [*indicating* PICKERING]: Tell him where he comes from, if you want to go fortune-telling.

HIGGINS: Cheltenham, Harrow, Cambridge, and India.

PICKERING: Quite right.

AND STILL ANOTHER BYSTANDER: Blimey, he ain't a tec; he's a bloomin' busybody, that's what he is!

[*The crowd starts leaving, highly impressed.*]

PICKERING: May I ask, sir, do you do this sort of thing for a living on the music halls?

[*All have gone except four* COSTERMONGERS *grouped about the smudge-pot fire,* HIGGINS, PICKERING, *and* ELIZA, *who is seated*

*on the kerb against one of the pillars arranging flowers and pitying
herself in murmurs.*]

HIGGINS: I have thought of that. Perhaps I will some day.

ELIZA: He's no gentleman, he ain't, to interfere with a poor
girl.

PICKERING: How do you do it, if I may ask?

HIGGINS: Simple phonetics. The science of speech. That's my profession, also my hobby. Anyone can spot an Irishman or a Yorkshireman by his brogue. I can place a man within six miles; I can
place him within two miles in London. [*Indicating* ELIZA] Some-
times within two streets.

ELIZA: Ought to be ashamed of himself, unmanly coward!

PICKERING: But is there a living in that?

HIGGINS: Oh, yes. Quite a fat one.

ELIZA: Let him mind his own business and leave a poor girl –

HIGGINS [*explosively*]: Woman! Cease this detestable boohooing
instantly or else seek the shelter of some other place of worship.

ELIZA [*with feeble defiance*]: I've a right to be here if I like, same as
you.

HIGGINS: A woman who utters such depressing and disgusting
sounds has no right to be anywhere – no right to live. Remember
that you are a human being with a soul and the divine gift of
articulate speech; that your native language is the language of
Shakespeare and Milton and the Bible; and don't sit there crooning
like a bilious pigeon.

ELIZA [*quite overwhelmed, looking up at him in mingled wonder and
deprecation without daring to raise her head*]: Aoooooooooooow!

HIGGINS:

Look at her – a pris'ner of the gutters;
Condemned by ev'ry syllable she utters.
By right she should be taken out and hung
For the cold-blooded murder of the English tongue!

ELIZA: A-o-o-o-w!

HIGGINS [*imitating her*]: Aoooow! Heavens, what a noise!

This is what the British population
Calls an element'ry education.

PICKERING: Come, sir, I think you picked a poor example.

HIGGINS: Did I?

Hear them down in Soho Square
Dropping aitches everywhere,
Speaking English any way they like.

[*To one of the* COSTERMONGERS *at the fire*]
You, sir, did you go to school?

COSTERMONGER:

Whatya tike me fer, a fool?

HIGGINS [*to* PICKERING]:

No one taught him 'take' instead of 'tike'.
Hear a Yorkshireman, or worse,
Hear a Cornishman converse.
I'd rather hear a choir singing flat.
Chickens cackling in a barn . . .

[*Pointing to* ELIZA]
Just like this one – !

ELIZA: – Garn!

HIGGINS:

Garn! I ask you, sir, what sort of word is that?
It's 'Aooow' and 'Garn' that keep her in her place.
Not her wretched clothes and dirty face.

Why can't the English teach their children how to speak?
This verbal class distinction by now should be antique.
If you spoke as she does, sir,
Instead of the way you do,
Why, you might be selling flowers, too.

PICKERING: I beg your pardon!

HIGGINS:

An Englishman's way of speaking absolutely classifies him.
The moment he talks he makes some other Englishman despise him.

One common language I'm afraid we'll never get.
Oh, why can't the English learn to set
A good example to people whose English is painful to your ears?
The Scotch and the Irish leave you close to tears.

There even are places where English completely disappears.
In America, they haven't used it for years!
Why can't the English teach their children how to speak?
Norwegians learn Norwegian; the Greeks are taught their Greek.
In France every Frenchman knows his language from 'A' to 'Zed'.
The French never care what they do, actually, as long as they
  pronounce it properly.

Arabians learn Arabian with the speed of summer lightning.
The Hebrews learn it backwards, which is absolutely frightening.
But use proper English, you're regarded as a freak.
Oh, why can't the English,
Why can't the English learn to speak?

[*He looks thoughtfully at* ELIZA] You see this creature with her kerb-stone English; the English that will keep her in the gutter to the end of her days? Well, sir, in six months I could pass her off as a duchess at an Embassy ball. I could even get her a place as a lady's maid or shop assistant, which requires better English.

ELIZA [*rising with sudden interest*]: Here, what's that you say?

HIGGINS: Yes, you squashed cabbage leaf, you disgrace to the noble architecture of these columns, you incarnate insult to the English language; I could pass you off as the Queen of Sheba.

PICKERING [*interested in* HIGGINS *but more so in finding a taxi, thinks he sees one and moves quickly to hail it*]: Taxi!

ELIZA: Aooow! [*To* PICKERING] You don't believe that, Captain?

PICKERING: Taxi! [*He loses the cab and comes back*] Oh, well, anything is possible. I myself am a student of Indian dialects.

HIGGINS [*eagerly*]: Are you? Do you know Colonel Pickering, the author of *Spoken Sanskrit*?

PICKERING: I am Colonel Pickering. Who are you?

HIGGINS: Henry Higgins, author of *Higgins' Universal Alphabet*.

PICKERING [*amazed*]: I came from India to meet you!

HIGGINS [*with enthusiasm*]: I was going to India to meet you!

PICKERING [*extending his hand*]: Higgins!

HIGGINS [*extending his*]: Pickering! [*They shake hands*] Where are you staying?

PICKERING: At the Carlton.

HIGGINS: No, you're not. You're staying at 27a Wimpole Street. Come with me and we'll have a jaw over supper.

PICKERING: Right you are. [*They start off together.*]

ELIZA [*to* HIGGINS *as they pass her*]: Buy a flower, kind sir. I'm short for my lodging.

HIGGINS [*shocked at the girl's mendacity*]: Liar! You said you could change half a crown.

ELIZA [*in desperation*]: You ought to be stuffed with nails, you ought. Here! [*Shoving her basket at him*] Take the whole bloomin' basket for sixpence!

[*The church clock strikes the second quarter.*]

HIGGINS [*he raises his hat solemnly*]: Ah. The church. A reminder. [*Throws a handful of money into the basket and follows* PICKERING] Indian dialects have always fascinated me. I have records of over fifty.

PICKERING: Have you, now. Did you know there are over two hundred?

HIGGINS: By George, it's worse than London. Do you know them all?

[*They disappear down the street.*]

ELIZA [*picking up a half-crown*]: Ah-ow-ooh! [*Picking up a couple of florins*] Aaah-ow-ooh! [*Picking up several coins*] Aaaaaaah-ow-ooh! [*Picking up a half-sovereign*] Aaaaaaaaaah-ow-ooh!! [*She skips to the fire to display her wealth.*]

FIRST COSTERMONGER [*with a sweep of his hat*]: Shouldn't you stand up, gentlemen? We've got a bloomin' heiress in our midst!

SECOND COSTERMONGER [*rises and clicking heels*]: Would you be
lookin' for a good butler, Eliza?

ELIZA [*haughtily*]: You won't do. [*She walks away.*]

SECOND COSTERMONGER:
>   *It's rather dull in town,*
>   *I think I'll take me to Paree.*

THIRD COSTERMONGER:
>   *The missus wants to open up*
>   *The castle in Capri!*

FIRST COSTERMONGER:
>   *Me doctor recommends*
>   *A quiet summer by the sea.*

THE FOUR:
>   *Mmmmmmmm! Mmmmmmm!*
>   *Wouldn't it be loverly!*

THIRD COCKNEY: Where're ya bound for this spring, Eliza?
Biarritz?

ELIZA [*leaning against the pillar*]:
>   *All I want is a room somewhere,*
>   *Far away from the cold night air;*
>   *With one enormous chair . . .*
>   *Oh, wouldn't it be loverly?*
>
>   *Lots of choc'late for me to eat;*
>   *Lots of coal makin' lots of heat;*
>   *Warm face, warm hands, warm feet . . . !*
>   *Oh, wouldn't it be loverly?*
>
>   *Oh, so loverly sittin' absobloominlutely still*
>   *I would never budge till spring*
>   *Crept over me winder sill.*
>
>   *Someone's head restin' on my knee,*
>   *Warm and tender as he can be,*
>   *Who takes good care of me . . .*

Oh, wouldn't it be loverly?
Loverly! Loverly!
Loverly! Loverly!

[*As* ELIZA *spins out her daydream, a few other* FLOWER GIRLS *and* VENDORS *are drawn on and stand silently listening. When she finishes, the four at the fire beguiled into the mood repeat the refrain as* ELIZA *and the others act out a dinner in an expensive restaurant: the ordering, the wine, the food — and riding home in a taxi afterwards. A dustcart serves the purpose. An icy blast blows across the market place bringing them quickly back to reality and they all gather around the fire and warm their hands.*]

SCENE TWO

Tenement section, Tottenham Court Road. A shabby back alley filled with atmosphere for everyone but those who live there. There is a small public house on one side of the stage, a converted mews on the other and, rising in the end of the street that divides the two, the misty outline of St Paul's Cathedral [Chris Wren's, not the Covent Garden St Paul's].

Time: Later that evening.

There is a commotion at the pub. GEORGE, *the bartender, is discovered forcibly evicting two disorderly members of the lowest possible class, by name* HARRY *and* JAMIE. GEORGE *now directs his remarks into the bar.*

BARTENDER: I ain't runnin' no charity bazaar. Drinks is to be paid for or not drunk. Come on, Doolittle. Out you go. Hop it now, Doolittle. On the double. On the double.

   [ALFRED DOOLITTLE *emerges. He is an elderly but vigorous dustman, clad in the costume of his profession, including a hat with a black brim covering his neck and shoulders. He has well-marked and rather interesting features, and seems equally free from fear and conscience. He has a remarkably expressive voice, the result of a habit of giving vent to his feelings without reserve. His present pose is that of wounded honour and casual disdain.*]

DOOLITTLE: Thanks for your hospitality, George. Send the bill to Buckingham Palace. [*The* BARTENDER *exits into pub as* DOOLITTLE *joins his associates*] Hyde Park to walk through on a fine spring night; the whole ruddy city of London to roam about in sellin' her bloomin' flowers. I give her all that, and then I disappears and leaves her on her own to enjoy it. Now if that ain't worth half a crown now and again, I'll take off my belt and give her what for.

JAMIE: You got a good heart, Alfie, but if you want that half a crown from Eliza, you better have a good story to go with it. [ELIZA *ambles on*.]

DOOLITTLE [*with paternal joy*]: Eliza! What a surprise!

ELIZA [*walking past him*]: Not a brass farthing.

DOOLITTLE [*grabbing her arm*]: Now you look here, Eliza. You wouldn't have the heart to send me home to your stepmother without a bit of liquid protection, now would you?

ELIZA: Stepmother. Ha! Stepmother, indeed!

DOOLITTLE: Well, I'm willing to marry her. It's me that suffers by it. I'm a slave to that woman, Eliza. Just because I ain't her lawful husband. [*Lovably*] Come on, Eliza, slip your old Dad half a crown to go home on.

ELIZA [*taking a coin from her basket, flipping it in air and catching it*]: Well, I had a bit of luck meself tonight. So here. [*Gives him coin.*]

HARRY [*jubilantly calls into pub*]: George! Three glorious beers!

ELIZA: But don't keep comin' around countin' on half-crowns from me! [*She disappears into the converted mews.*]

DOOLITTLE: Goodnight, Eliza! You're a noble daughter! [*He turns to his friends smugly*] You see, boys, I told you not to go home! It's just Faith, Hope, and a little bit of luck!

> *The Lord above gave man an arm of iron*
> *So he could do his job and never shirk.*
> *The Lord above gave man an arm of iron – but*
> *With a little bit of luck,*
> *With a little bit of luck,*
> *Someone else'll do the blinkin' work!*

THE THREE:

> *With a little bit ... with a little bit ...*
> *With a little bit of luck*
> *You'll never work!*

DOOLITTLE:

> *The Lord above made liquor for temptation,*
> *To see if man could turn away from sin.*

The Lord above made liquor for temptation – but
With a little bit of luck,
With a little bit of luck,
When temptation comes you'll give right in!

THE THREE:

With a little bit . . . with a little bit . . .
With a little bit of luck
You'll give right in.

DOOLITTLE:

Oh, you can walk the straight and narrow;
But with a little bit of luck
You'll run amuck!
The gentle sex was made for man to marry,
To share his nest and see his food is cooked.
The gentle sex was made for man to marry – but
With a little bit of luck,
With a little bit of luck,
You can have it all and not get hooked.

THE THREE:

With a little bit . . . with a little bit . . .
With a little bit of luck
You won't get hooked.
With a little bit . . . with a little bit . . .
With a little bit of bloomin' luck!

[*An* ANGRY WOMAN *pokes her head out of the upstairs window of the mews.*]

ANGRY WOMAN: Shut your face down there! How's a woman supposed to get her rest?

DOOLITTLE: I'm tryin' to keep 'em quiet, lady!

[*The voice of an* ANGRY MAN *is heard down the street.*]

ANGRY MAN: Shut up! Once and for all, shut up!

ANOTHER ANGRY MAN: One more sound, so help me, I'll call a copper!

DOOLITTLE: Here, here, here! Stop that loud talk! People are tryin' to sleep! [*He turns to his friends*] Let's try to be neighbourly-like boys. After all . . .

[*Sings softly*]

> The Lord above made man to help his neighbour,
> No matter where, on land, or sea, or foam.
> The Lord above made man to help his neighbour – but
> With a little bit of luck,
> With a little bit of luck,
> When he comes around you won't be home!

JAMIE AND HARRY:

> With a little bit . . . with a little bit . . .
> With a little bit of luck,
> You won't be home.

DOOLITTLE:

> They're always throwin' goodness at you;
> But with a little bit of luck
> A man can duck!
>
> Oh, it's a crime for man to go philanderin'
> And fill his wife's poor heart with grief and doubt
> Oh, it's a crime for man to go philanderin' – but
> With a little bit of luck,
> With a little bit of luck,
> You can see the bloodhound don't find out!

THE THREE [*at the top of their lungs*]:

> With a little bit . . . with a little bit . . .
> With a little bit of luck
> She won't find out!
> With a little bit . . . with a little bit . . .
> With a little bit of bloomin' luck!

[*Angry cries descend on them from all over the neighbourhood. They cheerfully disregard them and re-enter the pub.*]

SCENE THREE

HIGGINS' *study in Wimpole Street.*

It is a room on the first floor with one window in an alcove looking out on the street and double doors in the middle of the back wall. There is a balcony above them with stairs to one side leading up to it. There is another door on the balcony and the wall of the balcony is entirely covered with bookcases. Next to the door is a small table upon which is a recording machine and speaker horn.

There is a desk below the alcove upon which is a small bust of Plato, a mass of papers, several tuning forks of different sizes, and a telephone. Next to the desk is a small xylophone and another recorder and speaker. The alcove behind is a mass of filing cabinets and books. There is a bird cage containing a bird next to the window.

There is a sofa in the middle of the room, an easy chair next to the stairs, and a small stool in front of the desk. Behind the easy chair is another machine and, against the wall by the double doors, still another.

Time: The next day.

The room is dark. In the darkness between the scenes strange guttural sounds pour forth from the public address system. PICKERING *is seated in the easy chair.* HIGGINS *is standing by the recording machine next to his desk. The strange sounds heard in the darkness a moment before are now discovered to be coming from the recorder. When the lights go on, as they will in a moment,* HIGGINS *in the morning light is seen to be a robust, vital, appetizing sort of a man of forty or thereabouts. He is of the energetic scientific type, heartily, even violently, interested in everything that can be studied as a scientific subject, and careless about himself and other people, including their feelings. He is, in fact, but for his years and size, rather like a very impetuous baby 'taking notice' eagerly and loudly, and requiring almost as much watching to keep him out of unintended mischief. His*

29

manner varies from genial bullying when he is in a good humour to stormy petulance when anything goes wrong; but he is so entirely frank and void of malice that he remains likeable even in his least reasonable moments.

PICKERING: I say, Higgins, couldn't we turn on the lights?

HIGGINS: Nonsense, you hear much better in the dark.

PICKERING: But it's a fearful strain listening to all these vowel sounds. I'm quite done up for this morning.

[MRS PEARCE *enters. She is* HIGGINS' *housekeeper.*]

MRS PEARCE: Mr Higgins, are you there?

HIGGINS: What is it, Mrs Pearce? [*He turns down the volume of the machine.*]

MRS PEARCE: A young woman wants to see you, sir.

HIGGINS [*turning the machine off*]: A young woman! What does she want? [*He switches on the light.*] Has she an interesting accent? [*To* PICKERING] Let's have her up. Show her up, Mrs Pearce.

MRS PEARCE: Very well, sir. It's for you to say. [*She goes out into the hall.*]

HIGGINS: This is rather a bit of luck. I'll show you how I make records. We'll set her talking; and I'll take her down in Bell's Visible Speech; then in Broad Romic; and then we'll get her on the phonograph so that you can turn her on as often as you like with the written transcript before you.

MRS PEARCE [*returning*]: This is the young woman, sir.

[ELIZA *enters in state. She has a hat with three ostrich feathers, orange, sky-blue, and red. She has a nearly clean apron, and the shoddy coat has been tidied a little. The pathos of this deplorable figure, with its innocent vanity and consequential air, touches* PICKER-ING, *who has already straightened himself in the presence of* MRS PEARCE. *But as to* HIGGINS, *the only distinction he makes between men and women is that when he is neither bullying nor exclaiming to the heavens against some featherweight cross, he coaxes women as a child coaxes its nurse when it wants to get anything out of her.*]

HIGGINS [*brusquely, recognizing her with unconcealed disappointment, and at once, babylike, making an intolerable grievance of it*]: Why, this is the girl I jotted down last night. She's no use: I've got all the records I want of the Lisson Grove lingo, and I'm not going to waste another cylinder on it. [*To the girl*] Be off with you: I don't want you.

ELIZA: Don't be so saucy. You ain't heard what I come for yet. [*To* MRS PEARCE, *who is waiting at the door for further instructions.*] Did you tell him I come in a taxi?

MRS PEARCE: Nonsense, girl! What do you think a gentleman like Mr Higgins cares what you came in?

ELIZA: Oh, we are proud! He ain't above giving lessons, not him: I heard him say so. Well, I ain't come here to ask for any compliment; and if my money's not good enough I can go elsewhere.

HIGGINS: Good enough for what?

ELIZA: Good enough for ye-oo. Now you know, don't you? I'm come to have lessons, I am. And to pay for 'em too: make no mistake.

HIGGINS [*stunned*]: Well!!! [*Recovering his breath with a gasp*] What do you expect me to say to you?

ELIZA: Well, if you was a gentleman, you might ask me to sit down, I think. Don't I tell you I'm bringing you business?

HIGGINS: Pickering, shall we ask this baggage to sit down, or shall we throw her out of the window?

ELIZA [*running away in terror*]: Ah-ah-oh-ow-ow-ow-oo! [*Wounded and whimpering*] I won't be called a baggage when I've offered to pay like any lady!

PICKERING [*gently*]: What is it you want, my girl?

ELIZA: I want to be a lady in a flower shop, 'stead of selling at the corner of Tottenham Court Road. But they won't take me unless I can talk more genteel. He said he could teach me. Well, here I am ready to pay him – not asking any favour – and he treats me as if I was dirt. I know what lessons cost as well as you do; and I'm ready to pay.

HIGGINS: How much?

ELIZA [*coming back to him, triumphant*]: Now you're talking! I thought you'd come off it when you saw a chance of getting back a bit of what you chucked at me last night. [*Confidentially*] You'd had a drop in, hadn't you?

HIGGINS [*peremptorily*]: Sit down.

ELIZA: Oh, if you're going to make a compliment of it –

HIGGINS [*thundering at her*]: Sit down.

MRS PEARCE [*severely*]: Sit down, girl. Do as you're told.

PICKERING [*gently*]: What is your name?

ELIZA: Eliza Doolittle.

PICKERING: Won't you sit down, Miss Doolittle?

ELIZA [*coyly*]: Oh, I don't mind if I do. [*She sits down on sofa.*]

HIGGINS: How much do you propose to pay me for the lessons?

ELIZA: Oh, I know what's right. A lady friend of mine gets French lessons for heighteen pence an hour from a real French gentleman. Well, you wouldn't have the face to ask me the same for teaching me my own language as you would for French; so I won't give more than a shilling. Take it or leave it.

HIGGINS: You know, Pickering, if you consider a shilling, not as a simple shilling, but as a percentage of this girl's income, it works out as fully equivalent to sixty or seventy pounds from a millionaire. By George, it's the biggest offer I ever had.

ELIZA [*rising, terrified*]: Sixty pounds! What are you talkin' about? I never offered you sixty pounds! Where would I get . . .

HIGGINS: Oh, hold your tongue.

ELIZA [*weeping*]: But I ain't got sixty pounds. Oh . . .

MRS PEARCE: Don't cry, you silly girl. Sit down. Nobody is going to touch your money.

HIGGINS: Somebody is going to touch you with a broomstick, if you don't stop snivelling. Now, sit down.

ELIZA: Aoooow! One would think you was my father!

HIGGINS: If I decide to teach you, I'll be worse than two fathers to you. Here – [*He offers her his silk handkerchief.*]

ELIZA: What's this for?

HIGGINS: To wipe your eyes. To wipe any part of your face that feels moist. Remember, that's your handkerchief; and that's your sleeve. Don't mistake the one for the other if you wish to become a lady in a shop.

PICKERING: Higgins, I'm interested. What about your boast that you could pass her off as a duchess at the Embassy Ball? I'll say you're the greatest teacher alive if you can make that good. I'll bet you all the expenses of the experiment you can't do it. And I'll even pay for the lessons.

ELIZA: Oh, you're real good. Thank you, Captain.

HIGGINS [*tempted, looking at her*]: It's almost irresistible. She's so deliciously low – so horribly dirty!

ELIZA: Aoooow! I ain't dirty: I washed my face and hands afore I come, I did.

HIGGINS: I'll take it! I'll make a duchess of this draggle-tailed guttersnipe!

ELIZA: Aooooooow!

HIGGINS [*carried away*]: I'll start today! Now! This moment! Take her away and clean her, Mrs Pearce. Sandpaper if it won't come off any other way. Is there a good fire in the kitchen?

MRS PEARCE: Yes, but –

HIGGINS [*storming on*]: Take all her clothes off and burn them. Ring up and order some new ones. Wrap her up in brown paper till they come.

ELIZA: You're no gentleman, you're not, to talk of such things. I'm a good girl, I am; and I know what the likes of you are, I do.

HIGGINS: We want none of your slum prudery here, young woman. You've got to learn to behave like a duchess. Take her away, Mrs Pearce. If she gives you any trouble, wallop her.

ELIZA: I'll call the police, I will!

MRS PEARCE: But I've got no place to put her.

HIGGINS: Put her in the dustbin.

ELIZA: Aooooow!

PICKERING: Oh come, Higgins! Be reasonable.

MRS PEARCE: You must be reasonable, Mr Higgins, really you must. You can't walk over everybody like this.

[HIGGINS *thus scolded subsides. The hurricane is succeeded by a zephyr of amiable surprise.*]

HIGGINS [*with professional exquisiteness of modulation*]: I walk over everybody? My dear Mrs Pearce, my dear Pickering. I never had the slightest intention of walking over anybody. All I propose is that we should be kind to this poor girl. If I did not express myself clearly it was because I did not wish to hurt her delicacy, or yours.

MRS PEARCE: But, sir, you can't take a girl up like that as if you were picking up a pebble on the beach.

HIGGINS: Why not?

MRS PEARCE: Why not? But you don't know anything about her! What about her parents? She may be married.

ELIZA: Garn!

HIGGINS: There! As the girl very properly says: Garn!

ELIZA: Who'd marry me?

HIGGINS [*suddenly resorting to the most thrillingly beautiful low tones in his best elocutionary style*] : By George, Eliza, the streets will be strewn with the bodies of men shooting themselves for your sake before I've done with you.

ELIZA: Here! I'm goin' away! He's off his chump, he is. I don't want no balmies teachin' me.

HIGGINS [*wounded in his tenderest point by her insensibility to his elocution*]: Oh, indeed! I'm mad, am I? Very well, Mrs Pearce, you needn't order the new clothes for her. Throw her out! [*He deftly retrieves his handkerchief.*]

MRS PEARCE: Stop, Mr Higgins! I won't allow it. Go home to your parents, girl.

ELIZA: I ain't got no parents.

HIGGINS: There you are. 'She ain't got no parents.' What's all the fuss about? The girl doesn't belong to anybody, and she's no use to anybody but me. Take her upstairs and –

MRS PEARCE: But what's to become of her? Is she to be paid anything? Oh, do be sensible, sir.

HIGGINS [*impatiently*]: What on earth will she want with money? She'll have her food and her clothes. She'll only drink if you give her money.

ELIZA [*turning on him*]: Oh, you are a brute. It's a lie; nobody ever saw the sign of liquor on me. [*To* PICKERING] Oh, sir, you're a gentleman; don't let him speak to me like that!

PICKERING [*in good-humoured remonstrance*]: Does it occur to you, Higgins, that the girl has some feelings?

HIGGINS [*looking critically at her*]: Oh, no, I don't think so. Not any feelings that we need bother about. [*Cheerily*] Have you, Eliza?

MRS PEARCE: Mr Higgins. I must know on what terms the girl is to be here. What is to become of her when you've finished your teaching? You must look ahead a little, sir.

HIGGINS: What's to become of her if I leave her in the gutter? Answer me that, Mrs Pearce.

MRS PEARCE: That's her own business, not yours, Mr Higgins.

HIGGINS: Well, when I've done with her, we can throw her back into the gutter, and then it will be her own business again: so that's all right. [*He is moved to a chuckle by his own little pleasantry.*]

ELIZA: Oh, you've no feelin' heart in you: you don't care for nothing but yourself. Here! I've had enough of this. I'm going. [*She makes for the door.*]

HIGGINS [*taking her by the arm*]: Eliza! [*Snatching a chocolate cream from the table, his eyes suddenly twinkling with mischief*] Have some chocolates.

ELIZA [*halting, tempted*]: How do I know what might be in them? I've heard of girls being drugged by the like of you.

[HIGGINS *breaks the chocolate in two, puts one half into his mouth and bolts it.*]

HIGGINS: Pledge of good faith, Eliza. I eat one half and you eat the other. [ELIZA *opens her mouth to retort.* HIGGINS *pops the chocolate into it.*] You shall have boxes of them, barrels of them, every day. You shall live on them, eh?

ELIZA [*her mouth full*]: I wouldn't have ate it, only I'm too ladylike to take it out of me mouth.

HIGGINS [*taking her by the hand and leading her up the stairs*]: Think of it, Eliza. Think of chocolates, and taxis, and gold, and diamonds. [*They reach the balcony.*]

ELIZA: No! I don't want no gold and no diamonds. I'm a good girl, I am.

PICKERING: Excuse me, Higgins, but I really must interfere! Mrs Pearce is quite right. If this girl is to put herself in your hands for six months for an experiment in teaching, she must understand thoroughly what she's doing!

HIGGINS [*impressed with* PICKERING*'s logic, considers for a moment*]: Eliza, you are to stay here for the next six months learning how to speak beautifully, like a lady in a florist's shop. If you're good and do whatever you're told, you shall sleep in a proper bedroom and have lots to eat, and money to buy chocolates and take rides in taxis. If you're naughty and idle you will sleep in the back kitchen among the black beetles, and be walloped by Mrs Pearce with a broomstick. At the end of six months you shall go to Buckingham Palace in a carriage, beautifully dressed. If the King finds out you're not a lady, you will be taken by the police to the Tower of London where your head will be cut off as a warning to other presumptuous flower girls. If you are not found out, you shall have a present of seven-and-six to start life with as a lady in a shop. If you refuse this offer you will be the most ungrateful, wicked girl; and the angels will weep for you. [*To* PICKERING] Now are you satisfied, Pickering? [*To* MRS PEARCE] Could I put it more plainly or fairly, Mrs Pearce?

MRS PEARCE [*resigned, starts up the stairs*]: Come with me, Eliza.

HIGGINS: That's right, Mrs Pearce. Bundle her off to the bathroom.

ELIZA [*reluctantly and suspiciously*]: You're a great bully, you are. I won't stay here if I don't like. And I won't let nobody wallop me.

MRS PEARCE: Don't answer back, girl. [*She leads* ELIZA *through the door.*]

ELIZA [*as she goes*]: If I'd known what I was lettin' myself in for, I wouldn't have come up here. I've always been a good girl and I won't be put upon ... [*She follows* MRS PEARCE *out of the door.*]

HIGGINS [*coming down the stairs*]: In six months – in three if she has a good ear and a quick tongue – I'll take her anywhere and pass her off as anything. I'll make a queen of that barbarous wretch.

PICKERING: Higgins, forgive the bluntness, but if I'm to be in this business, I shall feel responsible for the girl. I hope it's clearly understood that no advantage is to be taken of her position.

HIGGINS: What? That thing? Sacred, I assure you.

PICKERING [*gravely*]: Now come, Higgins, you know what I mean! This is no trifling matter! Are you a man of good character where women are concerned?

HIGGINS: Have you ever met a man of good character where women are concerned?

PICKERING: Yes. Very frequently.

HIGGINS [*dogmatically*]: Well, I haven't. I find that the moment I let a woman make friends with me she becomes jealous, exacting, suspicious, and a damned nuisance. I find that the moment I let myself become friends with a woman, I become selfish and tyrannical. So here I am, a confirmed old bachelor, and likely to remain so. After all, Pickering ...

> *I'm an ordinary man;*
> *Who desires nothing more*
> *Than just the ordinary chance*
> *To live exactly as he likes*
> *And do precisely what he wants.*
> *An average man am I*
> *Of no eccentric whim;*
> *Who likes to live his life*
> *Free of strife,*

Doing whatever he thinks is best for him.
Just an ordinary man.

But let a woman in your life
And your serenity is through!
She'll redecorate your home
From the cellar to the dome;
Then get on to the enthralling
Fun of overhauling
You.

Oh, let a woman in your life
And you are up against the wall!
Make a plan and you will find
She has something else in mind;
And so rather than do either
You do something else that neither
Likes at all.

You want to talk of Keats or Milton;
She only wants to talk of love.
You go to see a play or ballet,
And spend it searching for her glove.

Oh, let a woman in your life
And you invite eternal strife!
Let them buy their wedding bands
For those anxious little hands;
I'd be equally as willing
For a dentist to be drilling
Than to ever let a woman in my life!

[With sudden amiability]
I'm a very gentle man;
Even-tempered and good-natured,
Whom you never hear complain;
Who has the milk of human kindness
By the quart in ev'ry vein.

A patient man am I
Down to my fingertips;
The sort who never could,
Ever would,
Let an insulting remark escape his lips.
A very gentle man.

   [Violently]
But let a woman in your life
And patience hasn't got a chance.
She will beg you for advice;
Your reply will be concise.
And she'll listen very nicely
Then go out and do precisely
What she wants!

You were a man of grace and polish
Who never spoke above a hush.
Now all at once you're using language
That would make a sailor blush.

Oh, let a woman in your life
And you are plunging in a knife!
Let the others of my sex
Tie the knot – around their necks;
I'd prefer a new edition
Of the Spanish Inquisition
Than to ever let a woman in my life!

   [The storm over, he 'cheeps' sweetly to the bird]
I'm a quiet living man
Who prefers to spend his evenings
in the silence of his room;
Who likes an atmosphere as restful
As an undiscovered tomb.

A pensive man am I
Of philosophic joys;
Who likes to meditate,
Contemplate,
Free from humanity's mad, inhuman noise.
Just a quiet living man.

   [*With abrupt rage*]
But let a woman in your life
And your sabbatical is through!
In a line that never ends
Come an army of her friends;
Come to jabber and to chatter
And to tell her what the matter
Is with you.

She'll have a booming, boist'rous fam'ly
Who will descend on you en masse.
She'll have a large Wagnerian mother
With a voice that shatters glass!

Oh, let a woman in your life . . .
[*He turns on one of the machines at the accelerated speed so that the voice coming over the speaker becomes a piercing female babble. He runs to the next machine*]
Let a woman in your life . . .
[*He turns it on the same way and dashes to the next*]
Let a woman in your life . . .
[*He turns on the third; the third being the master control, he slowly turns the volume up until the chattering is unbearable.* PICKERING *covers his ears, his face knotted in pain. Having illustrated his point,* HIGGINS *suddenly turns all the machines off and makes himself comfortable in a chair*] I shall never let a woman in my life!
[*The lights black out for the end of the scene.*]

SCENE FOUR

The tenement section, Tottenham Court Road, the same as Act One, Scene Two.

Time: Noon, three days later.

At rise of curtain: MRS HOPKINS, *a dishevelled Cockney lady, has been imparting some juicy gossip to a group of delighted neighbours. She is holding a bird cage and a Chinese fan.*

MRS HOPKINS: How'd ya like that? Knocked me for a row of pins, it did.

> [GEORGE, *the bartender, forcibly evicts* HARRY *and* JAMIE *and then calls into the pub.*]

GEORGE: Come on, Doolittle. Out you go. Hop it now. I ain't runnin' no charity bazaar.

DOOLITTLE [*coming from the pub*]: Thanks for your hospitality, George. Send . . .

GEORGE: Yes, I know. Send the bill to Buckingham Palace. [*He goes back into the pub.*]

MRS HOPKINS: You can buy your own drinks now, Alfie Doolittle. Fallen into a tub of butter, you have.

DOOLITTLE: What tub of butter?

MRS HOPKINS: Your daughter, Eliza. Oh, you're a lucky man, Alfie Doolittle.

DOOLITTLE: What are you talkin' about? What about Eliza?

MRS HOPKINS [*to the crowd*]: He don't know. Her own father, and he don't know. [*She and her friends have a good laugh at this.*] Moved in with a swell, Eliza has. Left here in a taxi all by herself, smart as paint, and ain't been home for three days. And then I gets a message from her this morning: she wants her things sent over

41

to 27a Wimpole Street, care of Professor Higgins. And what things does she want? Her bird cage, and her Chinese fan. [*She hands them to* DOOLITTLE] But, she says, never mind about sendin' any clothes! [*She, her friends, and* HARRY *and* JAMIE *laugh uproariously.* DOOLITTLE's *face shines with paternal pride and the prospect of prosperous days.*]

DOOLITTLE: I knowed she had a career in front of her! Harry, boy, we're in for a booze-up. The sun is shinin' on Alfred P. Doolittle!

> *A man was made to help support his children,*
> *Which is the right and proper thing to do.*
> *A man was made to help support his children – but*
> *With a little bit of luck,*
> *With a little bit of luck,*
> *They'll go out and start supporting you!*

ALL:

> *With a little bit . . . with a little bit . . .*
> *With a little bit of luck,*
> *They'll work for you.*
> *He doesn't have a tuppence in his pocket.*
> *The poorest bloke you'll ever hope to meet.*
> *He doesn't have a tuppence in his pocket – but*
> *With a little bit of luck,*
> *With a little bit of luck,*
> *He'll be movin' up to easy street.*
>
> *With a little bit . . . with a little bit . . .*
> *With a little bit of luck,*
> *He's movin' up.*
> *With a little bit . . . with a little bit . . .*
> *With a little bit of bloomin' luck!*

[*To the cheers of the crowd,* DOOLITTLE *trips gaily off, a man on the way to El Dorado.*]

SCENE FIVE

HIGGINS' *study*.

Time: Later that afternoon.

At rise of curtain: PICKERING *is seated in the wing chair, reading his paper.* MRS PEARCE *is standing near the desk holding some letters in her hand.* HIGGINS *is on the balcony engrossed in a bit of research.*

MRS PEARCE [*sternly*]: Mr Higgins, you simply cannot go on working the girl this way. Making her say her alphabet over and over, from sunup to sundown, even during meals – when will it stop?

HIGGINS [*detached but still logical*]: When she does it properly, of course. Is that all, Mrs Pearce?

MRS PEARCE: No, sir. The mail.

HIGGINS: Pay the bills and say no to the invitations.

MRS PEARCE: There's another letter from that American millionaire, Ezra D. Wallingford. He still wants you to lecture for his Moral Reform League.

HIGGINS: Throw it away.

MRS PEARCE [*not to be put off*]: It's the third letter he's written you, sir. You should at least answer it.

HIGGINS [*anything for peace*]: Oh, all right. Leave it on the desk. I'll get to it.

[MRS PEARCE *places the letter on the desk. While she is doing so, the* BUTLER *enters and addresses* HIGGINS *on the landing.*]

BUTLER: If you please, sir, there's a dustman downstairs, Alfred Doolittle, who wants to see you. He says you have his daughter here.

PICKERING [*coming to life*]: Phew! I say!

HIGGINS [*promptly*]: Send the blackguard up.

43

[*The* BUTLER *goes.*]

PICKERING: He may not be a blackguard, Higgins.

HIGGINS: Nonsense. Of course he's a blackguard.

PICKERING: Whether he is or not, I'm afraid we shall have some trouble with him.

HIGGINS [*confidently*]: Oh no, I think not. If there's any trouble he shall have it with me, not I with him.

[*The* BUTLER *returns.*]

BUTLER: Doolittle, sir.

[DOOLITTLE *enters and gravely addresses* PICKERING.]

DOOLITTLE: Professor 'iggins?

[*The* BUTLER *goes.*]

HIGGINS [*from the balcony*]: Here!

[DOOLITTLE *looks up, momentarily shaken.*]

DOOLITTLE: Morning, Governor. I come about a very serious matter, Governor.

HIGGINS [*to* PICKERING]: Born in Hounslow, mother Welsh! [*To* DOOLITTLE] What do you want, Doolittle?

DOOLITTLE [*menacingly*]: I want my daughter. That's what I want. See?

HIGGINS: Of course you do. You're her father, aren't you? I'm glad to see you have some spark of family feeling left. She's upstairs, here. Take her away at once.

DOOLITTLE [*fearfully taken aback*]: What??!!

HIGGINS: Take her away. Do you suppose I'm going to keep your daughter for you?

DOOLITTLE [*remonstrating*]: Now, now, look here, Governor. Is this reasonable? Is it fairity to take advantage of a man like this? The girl belongs to me. You got her. Where do I come in?

HIGGINS [*charging down the stairs*]: How dare you come here and attempt to blackmail me? You sent her here on purpose.

DOOLITTLE [*protesting*]: Now don't take a man up like that, Governor.

HIGGINS: The police shall take you up. This is a plant – a plot to

44

extort money by threats. I shall telephone the police. [*He goes resolutely to the telephone on the desk.*]

DOOLITTLE: Have I asked you for a brass farthing? I leave it to this gentleman here. [*To* PICKERING] Have I said a word about money?

HIGGINS: What else did you come for?

DOOLITTLE [*sweetly*]: Well, what would a man come for? Be human, Governor. [*He wheezes genially in* HIGGINS' *face and rocks him back several paces.*]

HIGGINS [*recovering*]: Alfred, you sent her here on purpose?

DOOLITTLE: So help me, Governor, I never did.

HIGGINS: Then how did you know she was here?

DOOLITTLE: I'll tell ya, Governor, if you'll only let me get a word in. I'm willing to tell ya. I'm wanting to tell ya. I'm waiting to tell ya.

HIGGINS: Pickering, this chap has a certain natural gift of rhetoric. Observe the rhythm of his native woodnotes wild: 'I'm willing to tell you; I'm wanting to tell you; I'm waiting to tell you.' That's the Welsh strain in him. [*To* DOOLITTLE] How did you know Eliza was here if you didn't send her?

DOOLITTLE: She sent back for her luggage, and I got to hear about it. She said she didn't want no clothes. What was I to think from that, Governor. I ask you as a parient, what was I to think?

HIGGINS: So you came to rescue her from worse than death, eh?

DOOLITTLE [*relieved at being so well understood*]: Just so, Governor. That's right.

HIGGINS: Mrs Pearce, Eliza's father has come to take her away. Give her to him.

DOOLITTLE [*desperately*]: Now wait a minute, Governor, wait a minute. You and me is men of the world, ain't we?

HIGGINS: Oh! Men of the world, are we? You'd better go, Mrs Pearce.

MRS PEARCE: I think so indeed, sir! [*She goes with dignity.*]

DOOLITTLE: Governor, I've taken a sort of fancy to you. [*Again he*

wheezes in HIGGINS' *face, causing the latter almost to lose balance*]
And if you want the girl I'm not so set on havin' her back home
again, but what I might be open to is an arrangement. All I ask is
my rights as a father; and you're the last man alive to expect me
to let her go for nothing; for I can see you're one of the straight
sort, Governor. Well, what's a five-pound note to you? And
what's Eliza to me?

PICKERING: I think you ought to know, Doolittle, that Mr Higgins'
intentions are entirely honourable.

DOOLITTLE [*to* PICKERING]: Of course they are, Governor. If I
thought they wasn't, I'd ask fifty.

HIGGINS [*revolted*]: Do you mean to say that you would sell your
daughter for fifty pounds?

PICKERING: Have you no morals, man?

DOOLITTLE [*frankly*]: No! I can't afford 'em, Governor. Neither
could you if you was as poor as me. Not that I mean any harm,
mind ya . . . but . . . if Eliza is going to get a bit out of this, why
not me, too? Eh? Look at it my way. What am I? I ask ya, what am
I? I'm one of the undeserving poor, that's what I am. Think what
that means to a man. It means he's up agenst middle-class morality
all the time. If there's anything going and I put in for a bit of it,
it's always the same story: you're undeserving, so you can't have
it. But my needs is as great as the most deserving widow's that
ever got money out of six different charities in one week for the
death of the same husband. I don't need less than a deserving man,
I need more. I don't eat less hearty than he does, and I drink a lot
more. I'm playing straight with you. I ain't pretending to be
deserving. I'm undeserving, and I mean to go on being undeserving. I like it, and that's the truth. But will you take advantage of
a man's nature to do him out of the price of his own daughter
what he's brought up, fed and clothed by the sweat of his brow,
till she's growed big enough to be interesting to you two gentlemen? Is five pounds unreasonable? I put it to you, and I leave it
to you.

HIGGINS: You know, Pickering, if we were to take this man in hand for three months, he could choose between a seat in the Cabinet and a popular pulpit in Wales. I suppose we ought to give him a fiver?

PICKERING: He'll make bad use of it, I'm afraid.

DOOLITTLE: Not me, so help me, Governor, I won't. Just one good spree for myself and the missus, givin' pleasure to ourselves and employment to others, and satisfaction to you to know it ain't been throwed away. You couldn't spend it better.

HIGGINS: This is irresistible. Let's give him ten. [*He goes to his desk for his wallet.*]

DOOLITTLE: No! The missus wouldn't have the heart to spend ten, Governor; ten pounds is a lot of money: it makes a man feel prudent-like; and then goodbye to happiness. No, you give me what I ask for, Governor: not a penny less, not a penny more.

PICKERING: I rather draw the line at encouraging this sort of immorality. Doolittle, why don't you marry that missus of yours? After all, marriage is not so frightening. You married Eliza's mother.

DOOLITTLE: Who told you that, Governor?

PICKERING [*stunned*]: Well, nobody told me. But I concluded naturally . . .

[DOOLITTLE *emphatically shakes his head to the contrary*.]

HIGGINS [*returning with a five-pound note*]: Pickering, if we listen to this man another minute we shall have no convictions left. Five pounds, I think you said?

DOOLITTLE [*taking it*]: Thank you, Governor.

[*He hurries for the door, anxious to get away with his booty. In the rush, he collides with a rather nicely dressed, clean, but angry young woman with a copy book in her hand. It is, of course,* ELIZA *whom he does not recognize.* MRS PEARCE *is with her*.]

ELIZA [*in a rage*]: I won't! I won't! I won't!

DOOLITTLE [*at the collision*]: Beg pardon, Miss!

ELIZA [*ignoring him and confronting* HIGGINS]: I won't say those ruddy vowels one more time!

DOOLITTLE: Blimey, it's Eliza! I never thought she'd clean up so good-lookin'. She does me credit, don't she, Governor?

ELIZA [*her anger heightened by his presence*]: Here! What are you doin' here?

DOOLITTLE [*sternly*]: You hold your tongue and don't you give these gentlemen none of your lip. If you have any trouble with her, Governor, give her a few licks of the strap. That's the way to improve her mind. [*He bows low*] Good mornin', gentlemen. [*Cheerfully whacking* ELIZA *on the backside*] Cheerio, Eliza. [*He goes out of the door in such high good spirits he cannot resist laughing out loud.*]

HIGGINS: By George, there's a man for you! A philosophical genius of the first water. Mrs Pearce, write to Mr Ezra Wallingford and tell him if he wants a lecturer to get in touch with Mr Alfred P. Doolittle, a common dustman – but one of the most original moralists in England.

MRS PEARCE: Yes, sir. [*She goes.*]

ELIZA: Here, what did he come for?

HIGGINS: Say your vowels.

ELIZA [*ready to explode at the mention of them*]: I know my vowels. I knew them before I came.

HIGGINS: If you know them, say them.

ELIZA: Ahyee, E, Iyee, Ow, You!

HIGGINS [*thundering*]: Stop! Say: A, E, I, O, U!

ELIZA: That's what I said: Ahyee, E, Iyee, Ow, You. I've been syin' them for three days, and I won't sy them no more!

PICKERING [*gently*]: I know it's difficult, Miss Doolittle. But try to understand . . .

HIGGINS: No use explaining, Pickering. As a military man you ought to know that. Drilling is what she needs. Much better leave her or she'll be turning to you for sympathy.

PICKERING: All right, if you insist, but have a little patience with her, Higgins. [*He goes out of the door.*]

1. Eliza *(Audrey Hepburn)*

2a. Eliza outside Covent Garden

2b. 'Why can't the English teach their children how to speak?' Professor
Higgins *(Rex Harrison)*, Eliza, and Colonel Pickering *(Wilfrid Hyde White)*

3a. 'Why can't a woman be more like a man?'

3b. 'The rain in Spain stays mainly in the plain'

4a. 'I could have danced all night' Eliza and Mrs Pearce *(Mona Washbourne)*

4b. Eliza at Ascot

5a. Eliza's début at the ball

5b. Eliza and Alfred Doolittle (Stanley Holloway)

6a. 'Get me to the church on time'

6b. 'Don't talk of love . . . show me!' Eliza and Freddie *(Jeremy Brett)*

7a. 'I've grown accustomed to her face'

7b. 'I washed my face and hands afore I come I did'

8. Alfred Doolittle

HIGGINS: Of course. [*To* ELIZA] Say 'A'.

ELIZA: You ain't got no heart, you ain't.

HIGGINS: 'A'.

ELIZA: Ahyee!

HIGGINS [*walks up the stairs saying 'A' with each step,* ELIZA *defiantly echoing 'Ahyee'. When he reaches the landing he addresses her with firm resolve*] Eliza, I promise you you will pronounce your vowels correctly before this day is out, or there'll be no lunch, no dinner, and no chocolates! [*He exits through the door on the landing, punctuating his threat with a slam of the door.*]

[ELIZA, *in a blind rage, slams her study book down on the floor and stamps on it.*]

ELIZA:

> Just you wait, 'enry 'iggins, just you wait!
> You'll be sorry but your tears'll be too late!
> You'll be broke and I'll have money;
> Will I help you? Don't be funny!
> Just you wait, 'enry 'iggins, just you wait!
>
> Just you wait, 'enry 'iggins, till you're sick,
> And you scream to fetch a doctor double-quick.
> I'll be off a second later
> And go straight to the the-atre!
> Oh ho ho, 'enry 'iggins, just you wait!
>
> Oooooooh 'enry 'iggins!
> Just you wait until we're swimmin' in the sea!
> Oooooooh 'enry 'iggins!
> And you get a cramp a little way from me!
>
> When you yell you're going to drown
> I'll get dressed and go to town!
> Oh ho ho, 'enry 'iggins!
> Oh ho ho, 'enry 'iggins!
> Just you wait!

One day I'll be famous! I'll be proper and prim;
Go to St James so often I will call it St Jim!
One evening the King will say: 'Oh, Liza, old thing,
I want all of England your praises to sing.
Next week on the twentieth of May
I proclaim Liza Doolittle Day!
All the people will celebrate the glory of you,
And whatever you wish and want I gladly will do.'

'Thanks a lot, King,' says I, in a manner well-bred;
'But all I want is 'enry 'iggins' 'ead!'
'Done,' says the King, with a stroke.
'Guard, run and bring in the bloke!'

Then they'll march you, 'enry 'iggins, to the wall;
And the King will tell me: 'Liza, sound the call.'
As they raise their rifles higher,
I'll shout: 'Ready! Aim! Fire!'
Oh ho ho! 'enry 'iggins!
Down you'll go! 'enry 'iggins!
Just you wait!!!

Blackout

[*The lights come up in the study.* ELIZA *is on the stool in front of the desk.* HIGGINS *is in the alcove repairing a metronome.* PICKERING *as usual is in the wing chair reading the London* Times.]

ELIZA: The rine in spine sties minely in the pline.

HIGGINS [*correcting her*]: The rain in Spain stays mainly in the plain.

ELIZA: Didn't I sy that?

HIGGINS: No, Eliza, you didn't 'sy' that. You didn't even 'say' that. [*He picks up a small burner and brings it down to the desk*] Every night before you get into bed, where you used to say your prayers, I want you to repeat: 'The rain in Spain stays mainly in the plain,' fifty times. You will get much further with the Lord if you learn not to offend His ears. Now for your 'H's. Pickering, this is going to be ghastly!

PICKERING: Control yourself, Higgins. Give the girl a chance.

HIGGINS [*patiently*]: Of course. No one expects her to get it right the first time. Watch closely, Eliza. [*He places the burner on the desk and lights the flame.*] You see this flame? Every time you say your aitch properly, the flame will waver. Every time you drop your aitch, the flame will remain stationary. That's how you will know you've done it correctly; in time your ear will hear the difference. Now, listen carefully; in Hertford, Hereford, and Hampshire, hurricanes hardly ever happen.

[ELIZA *sits down behind the desk.*]

Now repeat after me, In Hertford, Hereford, and Hampshire, hurricanes hardly ever happen.

ELIZA [*conscientiously*]: In 'ertford, 'ereford, and 'ampshire, 'urricanes 'ardly hever 'appen!

HIGGINS [*infuriated*]: No, no, no, no! Have you no ear at all?

ELIZA [*willingly*]: Should I do it over?

HIGGINS: No. Please, no! We must start from the very beginning. [*He kneels before the flame*] Do this: ha, ha, ha, ha. [*He rises.*]

ELIZA: Ha-ha-ha-ha. [*She looks up at him happily.*]

HIGGINS: Well, go on. Go on.

[ELIZA *continues.* HIGGINS *strolls casually over to* PICKERING, *leaving* ELIZA *to aspirate at the flame*]

Does the same thing hold true in India, Pickering; the peculiar habit of not only dropping a letter like the letter aitch, but using it where it shouldn't be? Like 'hever' instead of 'ever'? You'll notice some of the Slavic peoples when they learn to speak English have a tendency to that with their G's. They say 'linger' (soft g) instead of 'linger' (hard g); and then they turn around and say 'singer' (hard g) instead of 'singer' (soft g).

[PICKERING *had never thought about it and naturally is perplexed*] I wonder why that's so. I must look it up.

[HIGGINS *starts for the landing.* ELIZA, *by this time, is sinking fast from lack of oxygen.* PICKERING *notices her dying gasps and pulls* HIGGINS' *arm to call his attention to it.*]

[*Thinking which book to consult*]

Go on! Go on!

[*He continues up the stairs.* ELIZA *musters together one final 'HA' and blows out the flame. The room is plunged into darkness.*]

[*In the darkness, six* SERVANTS *emerge, and stand in a spotlight at the far end of the study.*]

SERVANTS:

> Poor Professor Higgins!
> Poor Professor Higgins!
> Night and day
> He slaves away!
> Oh, poor Professor Higgins!
> All day long
> On his feet;
> Up and down until he's numb;
> Doesn't rest;
> Doesn't eat;
> Doesn't touch a crumb!

[*The spotlight goes off. The* SERVANTS *disappear and the lights come up in the study.* PICKERING *is seated in his favourite chair with a large and fulsome tea-table before him.* ELIZA *is on the sofa.* HIGGINS *is standing by the xylophone, a cup in one hand, a xylophone mallet in the other. He taps out eight notes. 'How kind of you to let me come'.*]

HIGGINS: *Kind* of you, *kind* of you, *kind* of you. Now listen, Eliza. [*He plays them again*] How kind of you to let me come.

ELIZA: How kind of *you* to let me come.

HIGGINS [*puts down the mallet in despair and walks over to the tea-table*]: No! *Kind* of you. It's just like '*cup* of tea'. *Kind* of you – *cup* of tea. *Kind* of you – Say 'cup of tea'.

ELIZA [*hungrily*]: Cappatea.

HIGGINS: No! No! A cup of tea . . . [*Takes a mouthful of cake from the tray*] It's awfully good cake. I wonder where Mrs Pearce gets it?

PICKERING: Mmmmm! First rate! The strawberry tarts are delicious. And did you try the pline cake? [HIGGINS *looks at him in horror and then turns to* ELIZA.]

HIGGINS: Now, try it again, Eliza. A cup of tea. A cup of tea.

ELIZA [*longingly*]: A cappatea.

HIGGINS: Can't you hear the difference? Put your tongue forward until it squeezes against the top of your lower teeth. Now say 'cup'.

ELIZA [*her attention only on the cake in* HIGGINS' *hand*]: C-cup.

HIGGINS: Now say 'of'.

ELIZA: Of.

HIGGINS: Now say, cup, cup, cup, cup-of, of, of, of.

ELIZA: Cup, cup, cup, cup-of, of, of, of! Cup, cup, cup, cup-of, of, of, of . . .

PICKERING [*as she's practising*]: By Jove, that was a glorious tea, Higgins. Do finish the strawberry tart. I couldn't eat another thing.

HIGGINS: No, thanks, old chap, really.

PICKERING: It's a shame to waste it.

HIGGINS: Oh, it won't go to waste. [*He takes the last tart*] I know someone who's immensely fond of strawberry tarts.

[ELIZA's *eyes light up hopefully. But alas,* HIGGINS *walks right past her and goes to the bird cage.*]

HIGGINS [*pushing the cake through the bars*]: Cheep, cheep, cheep!

ELIZA [*shrieking*]: Aaaaaaaaaaaaooooooooooowwwww!!

Blackout

[*The lights black out and the* SERVANTS *again appear in the spotlight.*]

SERVANTS:

Poor Professor Higgins!
Poor Professor Higgins!
On he plods
Against all odds;
Oh, poor Professor Higgins!

Nine p.m.
Ten p.m.
On through midnight ev'ry night.
One a.m.
Two a.m.
Three . . .!

[*The spotlight goes off. The* SERVANTS *disappear and the lights come up again in the study.* ELIZA *is seated in the wing chair.* HIGGINS *has drawn up the stool and is facing her, a small box of marbles in his hand. He is placing them in her mouth.*]

HIGGINS: Four . . . five . . . six marbles. There we are. [*He holds up a slip of paper*] Now, I want you to read this and enunciate each word just as if the marbles were not in your mouth. 'With blackest moss, the flower pots were thickly crusted, one and all.' Each word clear as a bell. [*He gives her the paper.*]

ELIZA [*unintelligibly*]: With blackest moss the flower pots . . . I can't! I can't!

PICKERING [*from the sofa*]: I say, Higgins, are those pebbles really necessary?

HIGGINS: If they were necessary for Demosthenes, they are necessary for Eliza Doolittle. Go on, Eliza.

ELIZA [*trying again with no better results*]: With blackest moss, the flower pots were thickly crusted, one and all . . .

HIGGINS: I cannot understand a word. Not a word.

ELIZA [*her anger coming through the marbles and 'flower pots'*]: With blackest moss, the flower pots were thickly crusted, one and all; the rusted nails fell from the knots that held the pear to the gable-wall . . .

PICKERING [*soon after she has begun*]: I say, Higgins, perhaps the poem is too difficult for the girl. Why don't you try a simpler one, like: 'The Owl and the Pussycat'? Oh, yes, that's a charming one.

HIGGINS [*bellowing*]: Pickering! I cannot hear the girl!

[ELIZA *gasps and takes the marbles out of her mouth.*]

What's the matter? Why did you stop?

ELIZA: I swallowed one.

HIGGINS [*reassuringly*]: Oh, don't worry. I have plenty more. Open your mouth.

[*The lights go out and into the spotlight again appear the* SERVANTS.]

SERVANTS:

> *Quit, Professor Higgins!*
> *Quit, Professor Higgins!*
> *Hear our plea*
> *Or payday we*
> *Will quit, Professor Higgins!*
> *Ay not I,*
> *O not Ow,*
> *Pounding, pounding in our brain.*
> *Ay not I,*
> *O, not Ow,*
> *Don't say 'Rine,' say 'Rain' . . .*

[*The spotlight goes off. The* SERVANTS *disappear and the lights come up again in the study.* ELIZA *is draped wearily on the sofa.* PICKERING *is half asleep in the wing chair.* HIGGINS *is seated at his desk, an ice-bag on his head. The grey light outside the windows indicates the early hours of the morning.*]

HIGGINS [*wearily*]: The rain in Spain stays mainly in the plain.

ELIZA: I can't. I'm so tired. I'm so tired.

PICKERING [*half asleep*]: Oh, for God's sake, Higgins. It must be three o'clock in the morning. Do be reasonable.

HIGGINS [*rising*]: I am always reasonable. Eliza, if I can go on with a blistering headache, you can.

ELIZA: I have a headache, too.

HIGGINS: Here.

[*He plops the ice-bag on her head. She takes it off her head and buries her face in her hands, exhausted to the point of tears.*]

[*With sudden gentleness*] Eliza, I know you're tired. I know your head aches. I know your nerves are as raw as meat in a butcher's window. But think what you're trying to accomplish. [*He sits next to her on sofa.*] Think what you're dealing with. The majesty and grandeur of the English language. It's the greatest possession we have. The noblest sentiments that ever flowed in the hearts of men are contained in its extraordinary, imaginative, and musical mixtures of sounds. That's what you've set yourself to conquer, Eliza. And conquer it you will. [*He rises, goes to the chair behind his desk and seats himself heavily.*] Now, try it again.

ELIZA [*slowly*]: The rain in Spain stays mainly in the plain.

HIGGINS [*sitting up*]: What was that?

ELIZA: The rain in Spain stays mainly in the plain.

HIGGINS [*rising, unbelieving*]: Again.

ELIZA:

> *The rain in Spain stays mainly in the plain.*

HIGGINS [*to* PICKERING]:

> *I think she's got it! I think she's got it!*

ELIZA:

> *The rain in Spain stays mainly in the plain.*

HIGGINS [*triumphantly*]:

> *By George, she's got it!*
> *By George, she's got it!*
> *Now once again, where does it rain?*

ELIZA:

> *On the plain! On the plain!*

HIGGINS:

> *And where's that soggy plain?*

ELIZA: *In Spain! In Spain!*

[PICKERING *jumps to his feet and the three sing out joyously.*]

THE THREE:

> *The rain in Spain stays mainly in the plain!*
> *The rain in Spain stays mainly in the plain!*
> [HIGGINS *walks excitedly to the xylophone.*]

HIGGINS:

> *In Hertford, Hereford, and Hampshire . . .?*

ELIZA:

    Hurricanes hardly happen.

HIGGINS: [*taps out 'How kind of you to let me come'*]

ELIZA:

    How kind of you to let me come!

HIGGINS [*putting down the mallet and turning back to her*]

    Now once again, where does it rain?

ELIZA:

    On the plain! On the plain!

HIGGINS:

    And where's that blasted plain?

ELIZA:

    In Spain! In Spain!

THE THREE:

    The rain in Spain stays mainly in the plain!

    The rain in Spain stays mainly in the plain!

[*Joy and victory!* HIGGINS *takes a handkerchief from his pocket and waves it in front of* PICKERING *who charges it like the finest bull in Spain.* HIGGINS *turns and grabs* ELIZA *and they do a few awkward tango steps while* PICKERING *jumps around like a flamenco dancer shouting 'Viva Higgins, Viva.'* HIGGINS *swings* ELIZA *onto the sofa and joins* PICKERING *in a bit of heel-clicking.* ELIZA *jumps down from the sofa. They throw themselves into a wild jig and then all collapse back upon the sofa engulfed in laughter.*]

[MRS PEARCE *enters in her nightrobe, followed by two of the* SERVANTS *who have also been awakened.*]

HIGGINS: Pickering, we're making fine progress. I think the time has come to try her out.

MRS PEARCE [*making her presence known*]: Are you feeling all right, Mr Higgins?

HIGGINS: Quite well, thank you, Mrs Pearce. And you?

MRS PEARCE: Very well, sir, thank you.

HIGGINS: Splendid. [*To* PICKERING] Let's test her in public and see how she fares.

MRS PEARCE: Mr Higgins, I was awakened by a dreadful pounding. Do you know what it might have been?

HIGGINS: Pounding? I heard no pounding. Did you, Pickering?

PICKERING [*innocently*]: No.

HIGGINS: If this continues, Mrs Pearce, I should see a doctor. Pickering, I know! Let's take her to the races.

PICKERING [*rising*]: The races?

HIGGINS [*rising too, excited by the idea*]: Yes! My mother's box at Ascot.

PICKERING [*cautiously*]: You'll consult your mother first, of course.

HIGGINS: Of course. [*Thinking better of it*] No! We'll surprise her. Let's go straight to bed. First thing in the morning we'll go off and buy her a dress. Eliza, go on with your work.

MRS PEARCE: But Mr Higgins, it's early in the morning!

HIGGINS: What better time to work than early in the morning? [*To* PICKERING] Where does one buy a lady's gown?

PICKERING: Whiteley's, of course.

HIGGINS: How do you know that?

PICKERING: Common knowledge.

HIGGINS [*studying* PICKERING *carefully*]: We mustn't get her anything too flowery. I despise those gowns with a sort of weed here and weed there. Something simple, modest, and elegant is what's called for. Perhaps with a sash. [*He places the imaginary sash on* PICKERING'*s hip and steps back to eye it*] Yes. Just right.

[*He goes out of the door.* PICKERING *looks down at his hip to re-assure himself the sash is not there and follows after him.*]

[MRS PEARCE, *whose face has been a study in amazement, goes quickly to* ELIZA.]

MRS PEARCE: You've all been working much too hard. I think the strain is beginning to show. Eliza, I don't care what Mr Higgins says, you must put down your books and go to bed.

ELIZA [*lost on an errant cloud only hears her from far below*]:
Bed! Bed! I couldn't go to bed!
My head's too light to try to set it down!

Sleep! Sleep! I couldn't sleep tonight!
Not for all the jewels in the crown!

I could have danced all night!
I could have danced all night!
And still have begged for more.
I could have spread my wings
And done a thousand things
I've never done before.

I'll never know
What made it so exciting;
Why all at once
My heart took flight.
I only know when he
Began to dance with me,
I could have danced, danced, danced all night!

FIRST SERVANT [*to* ELIZA]:
It's after three, now.

SECOND SERVANT [*to* MRS PEARCE]:
Don't you agree, now,
She ought to be in bed?

[MRS PEARCE *nods emphatically.*]

ELIZA [*telling the servants*]:
I could have danced all night!
I could have danced all night!
And still have begged for more.
I could have spread my wings
And done a thousand things
I've never done before.

SERVANTS:
[*Simultaneously telling* ELIZA]
You're tired out.
You must be dead.
Your face is drawn,

59

Your eyes are red.
Now say goodnight, please.
Turn out the light, please.
It's really time
For you to be in bed.
Do come along.
Do as you're told,
Or Mrs Pearce
Is apt to scold.
You're up too late, miss.
And sure as fate, miss.
You'll catch a cold.

[MRS PEARCE *goes to the alcove for a comforter.*]

ELIZA:

I'll never know
What made it so exciting,
Why all at once
My heart took flight.
I only know when he
Began to dance with me
I could have danced, danced, danced all night!

SERVANTS:

[*Simultaneously*]
Put down your book
The work'll keep.
Now settle down
And go to sleep.

[ELIZA *stretches out on the sofa and* MRS PEARCE *covers her with a comforter.*]

MRS PEARCE:

I understand, dear.
It's all been grand, dear.
But now it's time to sleep.

[*She turns out the lights and she and the* SERVANTS *go.*]

ELIZA:

> [*Reliving it*]
> *I could have danced all night!*
> *I could have danced all night!*
> *And still have begged for more.*
> *I could have spread my wings*
> *And done a thousand things*
> *I've never done before!*
> *I'll never know*
> *What made it so exciting,*
> *Why all at once*
> *My heart took flight.*
>
> [*She throws off the comforter and jumps to her feet.*]
> *I only know when he*
> *Began to dance with me*
> *I could have danced, danced, danced all night!*

SCENE SIX

Near the race meeting, Ascot.

Time: A sunny June afternoon.

At rise of curtain: PICKERING, *dressed for Ascot, is strolling towards the club tent with* MRS HIGGINS. MRS HIGGINS, *elegantly gowned, is a woman a shade perhaps beyond sixty.* CHARLES, MRS HIGGINS' *chauffeur, follows dutifully behind.* MRS HIGGINS, *obviously perplexed by* PICKERING's *conversation, pauses.*

MRS HIGGINS: Colonel Pickering, I don't understand. Do you mean that my son is coming to Ascot today?

PICKERING: Yes, he is, Mrs Higgins. As a matter of fact, he's here!

MRS HIGGINS [*dismayed*]: What a disagreeable surprise. Ascot is usually the one place I can come to with my friends and not run the risk of seeing my son, Henry. Whenever my friends meet him, I never see them again.

PICKERING: He had to come, Mrs Higgins. You see, he's taking the girl to the annual Embassy Ball, and he wanted to try her out first.

MRS HIGGINS [*blank bewilderment*]: I beg your pardon?

PICKERING [*clearing it up*]: You know, the annual Embassy Ball.

MRS HIGGINS: Yes, I know the Ball; but what girl?

PICKERING: Oh, didn't I mention that?

MRS HIGGINS: No, you did not.

PICKERING: Well, it's quite simple, really. One night I went to the Opera at Covent Garden to hear one of my favourite operas, *Aida*; and as I was coming out ... Incidentally they didn't do *Aida* that night. No, they did *Götterdämmerung* instead. I'd never heard *Götterdämmerung*. By George, that's a rackety one! When the tenor chap ...

MRS HIGGINS [*impatiently*]: What about the girl, Colonel?

PICKERING: Oh, yes. As I was coming out, I met your son, Henry, who, in turn, met Miss Doolittle, who now lives with Henry.

MRS HIGGINS: Lives with Henry? [*Hopefully*] Is it a love affair?

PICKERING: Heavens no! She's a flower girl. He picked her up off the kerbstone.

MRS HIGGINS [*not quite believing her ears*]: A flower girl?

PICKERING: Yes. Higgins said to me: 'Pickering, you see this girl? In six months I could make a duchess of her.' I said: 'Nonsense.' He came right back with: 'Yes, I can.' 'All right,' I said, 'I'll make a bet with you you can't.' And I did. And he is.

MRS HIGGINS: But, Colonel, I still don't understand.

[*A distant bell is heard ringing.*]

CHARLES: The horses are leaving the paddock, Mrs Higgins.

PICKERING: Excuse me, Mrs Higgins. I must fetch her. [*He tips his hat politely and moves and starts off.*]

MRS HIGGINS: But Colonel, am I to understand that Henry is bringing a flower girl to Ascot?

PICKERING [*turning, delighted that* MRS HIGGINS *finally understands*]: Yes, Mrs Higgins! That's it, that's it precisely! Jolly good, Mrs Higgins! Jolly good!

MRS HIGGINS [*calmly*]: Charles, you'd better stay close to the car. I may be leaving abruptly. [*She sweeps off.*]

SCENE SEVEN

Scene: Inside a club tent, Ascot.

There is an archway in the centre and two large pouffes on either side. To view the races one would look out at the mythical 'fourth wall'.

Time: Immediately following.

At rise of curtain: The stage is filled with ladies and gentlemen of Ascot all appropriately attired for the occasion. At this precise moment, they are standing in groups looking out at the race track, the immobility of their faces and bodies registering their abiding disdain of any emotional display.

LADIES AND GENTLEMEN:
> *Ev'ry duke and earl and peer is here.*
> *Ev'ry one who should be here is here.*
> *What a smashing, positively dashing*
> *Spectacle: the Ascot op'ning day.*
>
> *At the gate are all the horses*
> *Waiting for the cue to fly away.*
> *What a gripping, absolutely ripping*
> *Moment at the Ascot op'ning day.*
> *Pulses rushing!*
> *Faces flushing!*
> *Heartbeats speed up!*
> *I have never been so keyed up!*
>
> *Any second now*
> *They'll begin to run.*
> *Hark! a bell is ringing,*
> *They are springing*
> *Forward*

Look! It has begun . . .!

[In stony silence and with a reserve indistinguishable from boredom they observe the progress of the race]

What a frenzied moment that was!

Didn't they maintain an exhausting pace?

'Twas a thrilling, absolutely chilling

Running of the Ascot op'ning race.

[To the strains of this Gavotte they move cautiously about, finally disappearing. MRS HIGGINS *enters and bows graciously to one or two as they go off. Almost immediately* HIGGINS *enters briskly, dressed in tweeds.]*

HIGGINS *[to himself]*: I don't know where the devil they could be. *[He sees his mother and comes to her]* Oh, darling, have you seen Pickering? My, you do look nice! *[Kisses her.]*

MRS HIGGINS: I saw Colonel Pickering, and Henry, dear, I'm most provoked. I've heard you've brought a common flower girl from Covent Garden to my box at Ascot.

HIGGINS: Oh, darling, she'll be all right. I've taught her to speak properly, and she has strict orders as to her behaviour. She's to keep to two subjects: the weather and everybody's health – sort of 'fine day' and 'how do you do', and not just let herself go on things in general. Help her along, darling, and you'll be quite safe.

MRS HIGGINS: Safe? To talk about our health in the middle of a race?

HIGGINS *[impatiently]*: Well, she's got to talk about something. *[His eyes wander about in search of them.]*

MRS HIGGINS: Henry, you're not even dressed properly.

HIGGINS: I changed my shirt.

MRS HIGGINS: Where is the girl now?

HIGGINS: Being pinned. Some of the clothes we bought for her didn't quite fit. I told Pickering we should have taken her with us.

MRS HIGGINS: You're a pretty pair of babies playing with your live doll.

*[*MRS EYNSFORD-HILL, FREDDY EYNSFORD-HILL, *and* LORD

and LADY BOXINGTON, *an elderly couple, stroll on.* MRS HIGGINS *greets them.*]

Ah, Mrs Eynsford-Hill!

HIGGINS: Oh damn, are all these people with you? [*He walks away.*]

MRS EYNSFORD-HILL: Mrs Higgins, is this your celebrated son?

MRS HIGGINS: I'm sorry to say my celebrated son has no manners. He may be the life and soul of the Royal Society soirées, but he's rather trying on more commonplace occasions.

[PICKERING *enters followed by* ELIZA, *who is exquisitely dressed; she produces an impression of remarkable distinction and beauty.*]

HIGGINS [*seeing them*]: Ah!

MRS HIGGINS: Ah, Colonel Pickering, you're just in time for tea.

PICKERING: Thank you. Mrs Higgins, may I introduce Miss Eliza Doolittle?

MRS HIGGINS [*extending her hand graciously*]: My dear Miss Doolittle.

ELIZA [*speaking with pedantic correctness of pronunciation and great beauty of tone*]: How kind of you to let me come. [*She says it properly and* HIGGINS *nods his approval.*]

MRS HIGGINS: Delighted, my dear. [*Introducing*] Mrs Eynsford-Hill. Miss Doolittle.

MRS EYNSFORD-HILL: How do you do?

ELIZA: How do you do? [*She gasps slightly in making sure of the H in 'how' but is quite successful.*]

MRS HIGGINS [*introducing*]: Lord and Lady Boxington. Miss Doolittle.

LORD AND LADY BOXINGTON: How do you do?

ELIZA: How do you do?

MRS HIGGINS [*introducing*]: And Freddy Eynsford-Hill.

ELIZA: How do you do?

FREDDY [*instantly infatuated*]: How do you do?

HIGGINS: Miss Doolittle?

ELIZA: Good afternoon, Professor Higgins.

[HIGGINS *motions for her to sit down, she looks at him blankly. He pantomimes sitting down and she does. They all seat themselves on the two pouffes,* ELIZA *finding herself between* MRS HIGGINS *and* FREDDY. HIGGINS, *of course, stays on his feet.* TWO STEWARDS *serve tea.*]

FREDDY: The first race was very exciting, Miss Doolittle. I'm so sorry you missed it.

MRS HIGGINS [*hurriedly*]: Will it rain do you think?

ELIZA: The rain in Spain stays mainly in the plain.

[HIGGINS *irresistibly does a quick fandango step which is so bizarre that the others have nothing to do but pretend it didn't happen*]

But in Hertford, Hereford, and Hampshire hurricanes hardly ever happen.

FREDDY: Ha, ha, how awfully funny.

ELIZA: What is wrong with that, young man? I bet I got it right.

FREDDY: Smashing!

MRS EYNSFORD-HILL: I do hope we won't have any unseasonably cold spells. It brings on so much influenza, and our whole family is susceptible to it.

ELIZA [*darkly*]: My aunt died of influenza, so they said. [MRS EYNSFORD-HILL *clicks her tongue sympathetically.*] But it's my belief they done the old woman in.

[HIGGINS *and* PICKERING *look at each other accusingly as if each blames the other for having taught* ELIZA *this last unrehearsed phrase.*]

MRS HIGGINS [*puzzled*]: Done her in?

ELIZA: Yes, Lord love you! Why should she die of influenza when she come through diphtheria right enough the year before? Fairly blue with it she was. They all thought she was dead; but my father, he kept ladling gin down her throat.

[HIGGINS, *for want of something to do, balances his tea cup on his head and takes several steps without spilling it. Quite a feat.*]

Then she came to so sudden that she bit the bowl off the spoon.

MRS EYNSFORD-HILL [*startled*]: Dear me!

ELIZA [*piling up the indictment*]: Now, what call would a woman with that strength in her have to die of influenza, and what become of her new straw hat that should have come to me? Somebody pinched it.

[HIGGINS *fans himself with a silver tray off the tea-cart*]

And what I say is, them as pinched it, done her in.

LORD BOXINGTON [*nervously loud*]: Done her in? Done her in, did you say?

HIGGINS [*hastily*]: Oh, that's the new small talk. To do a person in means to kill them.

MRS EYNSFORD-HILL [*to ELIZA, horrified*]: You surely don't believe your aunt was killed?

ELIZA: Do I not! Them she lived with would have killed her for a hatpin, let alone a hat.

MRS EYNSFORD-HILL: But it can't have been right for your father to pour spirits down her throat like that. It might have killed her.

ELIZA: Not her. Gin was mother's milk to her.

[PICKERING *stiffens.* HIGGINS *decides to leave, tips his hat to all, and starts off. However, his uncontrollable curiosity holds him at the last moment to hear what else ELIZA has to say.*]

Besides, he'd poured so much down his own throat that he knew the good of it.

LORD BOXINGTON: Do you mean that he drank?

ELIZA: Drank! My word! Something chronic. [*To FREDDY, who is in convulsions of suppressed laughter.*] Here! What are you sniggering at?

FREDDY: The new small talk. You do it so awfully well.

ELIZA: If I was doing it proper, what was you laughing at [*To HIGGINS*] Have I said anything I oughtn't?

MRS HIGGINS [*interposing*]: Not at all, my dear.

ELIZA: Well, that's a mercy, anyhow. [*Expansively*] What I always say is . . .

[PICKERING *jumps to his feet. He and* HIGGINS *make a number of desperate signals and strange sounds to prevent her from going on.*]

PICKERING [*rushing to* ELIZA]: I don't suppose there's enough time before the next race to place a bet? [*To* ELIZA] Come, my dear.

[ELIZA *rises*.]

MRS HIGGINS: I'm afraid not, Colonel Pickering.

[*They all rise as several of the ladies and gentlemen enter to take their positions for the next race.*]

FREDDY: I have a bet on number seven. I should be so happy if you would take it. You'll enjoy the race ever so much more.

[*He offers her a race ticket. She accepts.*]

ELIZA: That's very kind of you.

[FREDDY *leads* ELIZA *to a vantage point directly centre.*]

FREDDY: His name is Dover.

ELIZA [*repeating the name*]: Dover.

LADIES *and* GENTLEMEN *and* ALL [*except* HIGGINS]:

> There they are again
> Lining up to run.
> Now they're holding steady,
> They are ready
> For it.
> Look! It has begun!

[*Again the mummified silence. The one exception is* ELIZA. *Clenching her fists with excitement, she leans forward. Oblivious to the deportment of those around her, she begins to cheer her horse on.*]

ELIZA [*at first softly*]: Come on, come on, Dover!

[*The* LADIES *and* GENTLEMEN *slowly turn to stare at her and look at each other in wonder*]

Come on, come on, Dover!

[*Her voice crescendoes. The* LADIES *and* GENTLEMEN *move perceptively away from this ugly exhibition of natural behaviour*]

Come on, Dover!!! Move your bloomin' arse!!!

[*An agonizing moan rises from the crowd. The moment she says it she realizes what she has done and brings her hand to her mouth as if trying to push the words back in. Several women gracefully faint, and are caught by their escorts.* LORD *and* LADY BOXINGTON *are staggered.* PICKERING *flies from the scene running faster than Dover.* HIGGINS, *of course, roars with laughter.*]

SCENE EIGHT

Outside HIGGINS' *house, Wimpole Street.*
   Time: Later that day.
   At rise of curtain: A CONSTABLE *is strolling along the street.* FREDDY, *a man with a purpose, walks up to the* CONSTABLE.

FREDDY: Officer, I know this is Wimpole Street, but could you tell me where 27a is?

POLICEMAN [*indicating* HIGGINS' *house*]: Right there, sir.

FREDDY: Thank you. [*The* CONSTABLE *strolls on.* FREDDY *starts for the door when a* FLOWER GIRL *passes, looking very much as* ELIZA *used to, carrying a basket of flowers.* FREDDY *stops her.*] Are those for sale?

FLOWER GIRL: Yes, sir, A shilling.
   [FREDDY *takes a shilling from his pocket – his last – and gives it to the* FLOWER GIRL *in exchange for a small nosegay.*]

FREDDY: Here.

FLOWER GIRL: Thank you kindly, sir.

FREDDY [*with radiant good spirits*]: Isn't it a heavenly day?
   [*The* FLOWER GIRL *looks up at the sky which is quite overcast. Thinking him undoubtedly mad, she hurries on.*]
   [FREDDY *knocks on* HIGGINS' *door and while awaiting response, irrepressibly gives vent to his feelings.*]

FREDDY:
   When she mentioned how her aunt bit off the spoon,
   She completely done me in.
   And my heart went on a journey to the moon,
   When she told about her father and the gin.
   And I never saw a more enchanting farce,

Than the moment when she shouted 'move your bloomin' . . .'

MRS PEARCE [*opens the door*]: Yes, sir?

FREDDY: Is Miss Doolittle at home?

MRS PEARCE: Who shall I say is calling?

FREDDY: Freddy Eynsford-Hill. If she doesn't remember me, tell her I'm the chap who was sniggering at her.

MRS PEARCE [*looking at him strangely*]: Yes, sir.

FREDDY: And would you give her these? [*Hands her the nosegay.*]

MRS PEARCE: Yes, sir. [*She takes them and moves quickly to get the door between her and this odd young man.*]

FREDDY: You needn't rush. [*Gazing lovingly down the street*] I want to drink in this street where she lives.

MRS PEARCE: Yes, sir. [*She goes into the house.*]

FREDDY:

> *I have often walked down this street before;*
> *But the pavement always stayed beneath my feet before.*
> *All at once am I*
> *Several stories high,*
> *Knowing I'm on the street where you live.*
>
> *Are there lilac trees in the heart of town?*
> *Can you hear a lark in any other part of town?*
> *Does enchantment pour*
> *Out of ev'ry door?*
> *No, it's just on the street where you live!*
>
> *And oh! the towering feeling*
> *Just to know somehow you are near!*
> *The overpowering feeling*
> *That any second you may suddenly appear!*
> *People stop and stare. They don't bother me.*
> *For there's nowhere else on earth that I would rather be.*
> *Let the time go by,*
> *I won't care if I*
> *Can be here on the street where you live.*

[MRS PEARCE *opens the door.*]

MRS PEARCE [*cautiously*]: Mr Eynsford-Hill?

FREDDY: Yes?

MRS PEARCE: I'm terribly sorry, sir. Miss Doolittle says she doesn't want to see anyone ever again.

FREDDY: But why? She was magnificent!

MRS PEARCE: Magnificent? [*Not believing her ears*] Do you have the right address, sir?

FREDDY [*with calm resolution*]: Of course. Tell her I'll wait.

MRS PEARCE: But it might be days, sir. Even weeks!

FREDDY: But don't you see? I'll be happier here.

[MRS PEARCE *hastily goes back into the house.*]

FREDDY:

> People stop and stare. They don't bother me.
> For there's nowhere else on earth that I would rather be.
> Let the time go by,
> I won't care if I
> Can be here on the street where you live.

[FREDDY *settles himself down on the doorstep for the long wait.*]

SCENE NINE

HIGGINS' *study. There is a decanter of port and two glasses on the desk, next to them a carnation.*

Time: Evening. Six weeks later.

At rise of curtain: HIGGINS, *in white tie, is pacing slowly up and down the room, thoughtfully detached.* PICKERING, *also formally dressed, is obviously nervous.*

PICKERING: Higgins, if there's any mishap at the Embassy tonight, if Miss Doolittle suffers any embarrassment whatever, it's on your head alone. I've been begging you to call off this experiment ever since Ascot.

HIGGINS [*calmly*]: Eliza can do anything. [*He continues his stroll.*]

PICKERING: But suppose she's discovered? Suppose she makes another ghastly mistake?

HIGGINS [*good-humouredly*]: There'll be no horses at the Ball, Pickering.

PICKERING [*in a panic*]: But think how agonizing it would be! God, if anything happened tonight, I don't know what I'd do.

HIGGINS [*helpfully*]: You could always rejoin your regiment.

PICKERING [*exploding*]: Higgins, this is no time for flippancy. The way you've driven her these last six weeks has exceeded all the bounds of common . . . Oh, for God's sake, Higgins, stop pacing up and down! Can't you settle somewhere?

HIGGINS: Have some port. It will quieten your nerves.

PICKERING: I'm not nervous! Where is it?

HIGGINS: On the desk.

[PICKERING *goes to it and helps himself to a glass.*]
[MRS PEARCE *comes out of the door on the landing.*]

74

MRS PEARCE: The car is here, sir.

HIGGINS: Thank you, Mrs Pearce. Are you helping Eliza?

MRS PEARCE: Yes, sir. [*She goes.*]

PICKERING: Help her, indeed! I'll bet the damned gown doesn't fit. I warned you about those French designers. You should have gone to a good English store, where you knew everybody was on our side. Have a little port.

HIGGINS: No, thank you.

PICKERING: It will quieten your nerves.

HIGGINS [*still pacing*]: No, thank you.

PICKERING [*exasperated*]: Are you so sure she'll retain all you've hammered into her?

HIGGINS: We shall see.

PICKERING: But suppose she doesn't?

HIGGINS: Then I lose my bet. [*He settles himself comfortably on the sofa.*]

PICKERING [*slightly irritated*]: You know what I can't stand about you, Higgins? It's your confounded complacency. In a moment like this, with so much at stake, it's utterly indecent that you don't need a little port. What of the girl? You act as if she doesn't matter at all.

HIGGINS: Rubbish, Pickering. Of course she matters. What do you think I've been doing all these months? What could possibly matter more than to take a human being and change her into a different human being by creating a new speech for her? Why, it's filling up the deepest gulf that separates class from class, and soul from soul. She matters immensely.

[ELIZA *appears on the landing – a vision. She walks down the stairs and into the room.* HIGGINS *rises.* PICKERING *is overcome by her appearance.* HIGGINS *circles her inspecting her carefully.*]

PICKERING: Miss Doolittle, you look beautiful.

ELIZA: Thank you, Colonel Pickering.

PICKERING: Don't you think so, Higgins?

[ELIZA *turns to* HIGGINS *hopefully.*]

HIGGINS [*having decided the gown is quite all right*]: Not bad. Not bad at all.

[*The* BUTLER *and* FOOTMAN *enter with coats, hats, and* ELIZA's *cape and help each into his.* HIGGINS *goes to the desk for his carnation which he slips into his buttonhole, then looking furtively around to make certain* PICKERING *doesn't see him, he pours himself a quick glass of port. He starts briskly for the door. At the threshold, he pauses, turns, and gazes at* ELIZA. *He returns to her and offers his arm. She takes it and they go out of the door,* PICKERING *following after.*]

SCENE TEN

The Promenade outside the ballroom of the Embassy.

  Time: Later that evening.

  At rise of curtain: A FOOTMAN *is on the landing announcing the guests as the names are given to him from a* FOOTMAN *above. The promenade is filled with couples, some strolling on, some engaged in conversation with others.* MRS HIGGINS *is chatting with friends.*

FOOTMAN: Sir Reginald and Lady Tarrington.

  [SIR REGINALD *and* LADY TARRINGTON *descend the stairs and join friends in the room.*]

FOOTMAN: Professor Zoltan Karpathy.

  [KARPATHY *comes into the room. He is an important-looking man with an astonishingly hairy face. He has an enormous moustache flowing out into luxuriant whiskers. His hair glows with oil. He is wearing several worthless orders. Obviously a foreigner, one would guess him as Hungarian in which case one would be right. In spite of the ferocity of his moustache, he is amiable and genially voluble. He joins some friends.*]

FOOTMAN: Colonel Hugh Pickering.

  [PICKERING *enters looking about for* MRS HIGGINS. *Seeing her, he goes to her.*]

PICKERING: Mrs Higgins!

MRS HIGGINS [*to her group*]: Excuse me. [*She and* PICKERING *separate themselves.*]

PICKERING: Well, she got by the first hurdle. [*With muffled excitement*] The Ambassador's wife was completely captivated.

MRS HIGGINS: I know. I've heard several people asking who she is. Do tell me what happened.

PICKERING: Higgins said: 'Madam Ambassador, may I introduce Miss Eliza Doolittle?' and Madam Ambassador said: 'How do you do?' And Eliza came right back with: 'How do you do?'

MRS HIGGINS [*disappointed*]: Is that all?

PICKERING: Oh, no! When it was my turn, both the Ambassador and his wife said to me: 'Colonel Pickering, who is that captivating creature with Professor Higgins?'

MRS HIGGINS: What did you say?

PICKERING: Well, I was stopped for a moment. Then I collected myself and I said: 'Eliza Doolittle'.

MRS HIGGINS [*with sardonic appreciation*]: That was very quick thinking, Colonel.

PICKERING [*puffing up*]: Thank you. Mrs Higgins, do you think Eliza will make it?

MRS HIGGINS: Oh, I hope so! I've grown terribly fond of that girl.

FOOTMAN: Professor Henry Higgins.

[HIGGINS *appears on landing.* KARPATHY, *hearing his name, turns. As* HIGGINS *descends into the room,* KARPATHY *flings his arms wide apart and approaches him enthusiastically.*]

KARPATHY: Ah, maestro! Maestro! [*He kisses* HIGGINS *on both cheeks.*]

HIGGINS [*surprised, annoyed, and wounded by the whiskers*]: Oh! Oh!

KARPATHY: You remember me?

HIGGINS: No, I don't. Who the devil are you?

KARPATHY: I am your pupil, your first, best, and greatest pupil. I am Zoltan Karpathy, that marvellous boy. I have made your name famous throughout Europe. You teach me phonetics. You cannot forget me.

HIGGINS: Why don't you shave?

KARPATHY: I have not your imposing appearance; your figure, your brow. Nobody notice me when I shave.

HIGGINS [*noticing his chest full of medals*]: Where did you find all those old coins?

KARPATHY [*not at all offended – he can't be*]: Decorations for language.

The Queen of Transylvania is here this evening. I am indispensable to her at these international parties. I speak thirty-two languages. I know everybody in Europe. No impostor escape my detection. And now, Professor, you must introduce me to this glorious creature you escort this evening. She fascinate everyone Not since Mrs Langtry came to London ...

FOOTMAN: His Excellency Dr Themistocles Stephanos.

[*A well-decorated gentleman and his lady descend the stairs and join a group.*]

KARPATHY [*lowering his voice*]: This so-called Greek diplomat pretends he cannot speak English. But he does not deceive me. He is the son of a Yorkshire watchmaker. He speaks English so villainously that he dare not utter a word of it without betraying his origin. I help him to pretend, but I make him pay through the nose. I make them all pay. [*He irritatingly strokes* HIGGINS' *lapel*] I look forward to meeting your lady. [*He bows, a bit too low, and rejoins his group.*]

[PICKERING, *who has overheard this conversation, is in a state when* HIGGINS *goes to him.*]

PICKERING: Higgins, I say!

MRS HIGGINS [*nervously*]: Where's Eliza?

HIGGINS: Upstairs. Last-minute adjustment.

PICKERING: I say, Higgins, let's not risk it. Let's collect her and leave immediately.

MRS HIGGINS: Henry, do you think it wise to stay?

HIGGINS: Stay? Why not?

FOOTMAN: Miss Eliza Doolittle.

[ELIZA *descends the stairs.* HIGGINS *crosses to join her at the foot. Everyone turns and everyone stares.* KARPATHY *immediately comes forward.*]

KARPATHY: Ah, Professor, you must introduce me ...

[*He is interrupted by the strains of a regal march as the* QUEEN OF TRANSYLVANIA *and* CONSORT *make their grand entrance into the room. He retreats and joins in the mass bowing. As the* QUEEN *passes*

ELIZA *she is caught by her loveliness and places her hand lightly on her cheek.*]

QUEEN: Charming. Charming.

[*The* QUEEN *and* CONSORT *proceed to the ballroom as everyone rises to follow.*]

SCENE ELEVEN

The Ballroom of the Embassy. Sumptuous. Decorous.

Time: Immediately following.

Everyone has followed the QUEEN *into the ballroom. The waltz begins.* PROFESSOR KARPATHY *comes forward again and bows to* HIGGINS, *inviting an introduction.* HIGGINS *bows cheerfully in return, takes* ELIZA *in his arms, and dances away with her.*

KARPATHY, *now suspicious indeed, walks away. Slowly, the ballroom fills with couples whirling about in three-quarter time.* ELIZA *and* HIGGINS *dance off. Everyone changes partners and* ELIZA *returns in the arms of another.* KARPATHY *dances his partner closer and closer to her. When partners are changed again,* ELIZA *finds herself dancing with* KARPATHY. *Inaudibly because of the music,* KARPATHY *leads her into animated conversation; so animated, in fact, they stop dancing as the others continue waltzing around them.*

PICKERING *enters and sees them. He frantically waves across the room to attract* HIGGIN'S *attention.* HIGGINS *comes forward.* PICKERING, *by gestures, entreats* HIGGINS *to interrupt* KARPATHY *and* ELIZA; *but* HIGGINS, *regarding this as the ultimate test, decides to do nothing but watch and see what will happen.*

The curtain descends slowly.

✼✼✼✼✼✼✼✼✼✼✼✼

ACT TWO

✼✼✼✼✼✼✼✼✼✼✼✼

SCENE ONE

HIGGINS' *study*.

   Time: 3.00 the following morning.

   At rise of curtain: The SERVANTS, *having tried to stay awake to learn the outcome of the ball, have lost their battle with sleep, and are in various positions of oblivion in the room. The clock strikes 3.* MRS PEARCE *enters to awaken them as the sounds of voices are heard in the outside hall. They jump to their feet as* HIGGINS *and* PICKERING *enter.*

   ELIZA *follows. She is tired. Her expression is almost tragic. Seemingly unnoticed by all, she walks to the corner of the room and stands motionless by the desk as the two* FOOTMEN *help* PICKERING *and* HIGGINS *off with their cloaks.*

PICKERING [*jubilant*]: Higgins, it was an immense achievement.

HIGGINS [*yawning*]: A silly notion. If I hadn't backed myself to do it, I should have chucked the whole thing up two months ago.

PICKERING: Absolutely fantastic.

HIGGINS: A lot of tomfoolery.

PICKERING: Higgins, I salute you.

HIGGINS: Nonsense, the silly people don't know their own silly business.

PICKERING:
     Tonight, old man, you did it!
     You did it! You did it!
     You said that you would do it,
     And indeed you did.
     I thought that you would rue it;
     I doubted you'd do it.

> But now I must admit it
> That succeed you did.
> You should get a medal
> Or be even made a knight.

HIGGINS:

> It was nothing. Really nothing.

PICKERING:

> All alone you hurdled
> Ev'ry obstacle in sight.

HIGGINS:

> Now, wait! Now, wait!
> Give credit where it's due.
> A lot of glory goes to you.

[ELIZA *flinches violently but they take no notice of her. She recovers herself and stands stonily as before.*]

PICKERING:

> But you're the one who did it,
> Who did it, who did it!
> As sturdy as Gibraltar,
> Not a second did you falter.
> There's no doubt about it,
> You did it!

[*To* MRS PEARCE]

> I must have aged a year tonight.
> At times I thought I'd die of fright.
> Never was there a momentary lull.

HIGGINS [*lighting a cigar*]:

> Shortly after we came in
> I saw at once we'd eas'ly win;
> And after that I found it deadly dull.

PICKERING [*to* MRS PEARCE *and* MAIDS]:

> You should have heard the ooh's and ah's;
> Ev'ry one wond'ring who she was.

HIGGINS:

> *You'd think they'd never seen a lady before.*

PICKERING:

> *And when the Prince of Transylvania*
> *Asked to meet her,*
> *And gave his arm to lead her to the floor . . .!*

> [*To* HIGGINS]

> *I said to him: You did it!*
> *You did it! You did it!*
> *They thought she was ecstatic*
> *And so damned aristocratic,*
> *And they never knew*
> *That you*
> *Did it!*

> [ELIZA's *beauty becomes murderous.*]

HIGGINS: Thank Heavens for Zoltan Karpathy. If it weren't for him I would have died of boredom. He was there, all right. And up to his old tricks.

MRS PEARCE: Karpathy? That dreadful Hungarian? Was he there?

HIGGINS: Yes. [*The* SERVANTS *gather around him, hanging on every word*]

> [*In his best dramatic manner.*]

> *That blackguard who uses the science of speech*
> *More to blackmail and swindle than teach;*
> *He made it the devilish business of his*
> *'To find out who this Miss Doolittle is.'*
> *Ev'ry time we looked around*
> *There he was, that hairy hound*
> *From Budapest.*
> *Never leaving us alone,*
> *Never have I ever known*
> *A ruder pest.*
> *Fin'lly I decided it was foolish*
> *Not to let him have his chance with her*
> *So I stepped aside and let him dance with her.*

Oozing charm from ev'ry pore,
He oiled his way around the floor.
Ev'ry trick that he could play,
He used to strip her mask away.
And when at last the dance was done
He glowed as if he knew he'd won!
And with a voice too eager,
And a smile too broad,
He announced to the hostess
That she was a fraud!

MRS PEARCE: No!

HIGGINS: Yavol!

Her English is too good, he said,
Which clearly indicates that she is foreign.
Whereas others are instructed in their native language
English people aren.
And although she may have studied with an expert
Di'lectician and grammarian,
I can tell that she was born Hungarian!

[*He and* PICKERING *roar with laughter*]

Not only Hungarian, but of royal blood, she is a princess!

[*The* SERVANTS *can no longer contain their admiration.*]

SERVANTS:

Congratulations, Professor Higgins,
For your glorious victory!
Congratulations, Professor Higgins!
You'll be mentioned in history!

[HIGGINS *accepts this spontaneous demonstration graciously. He seats himself on the sofa and modestly puffs his cigar.*]

FOOTMAN:

This evening, sir, you did it!
You did it! You did it!
You said that you would do it!
And indeed you did.

THE REST OF THE SERVANTS:

Congratulations,
Professor Higgins!
For your glorious
Victory!

This evening, sir, you did it!   *Congratulations,*
You did it! You did it!   *Professor Higgins!*
We know that we have said it,   *Sing a hail and halleluia*
But – you did it and the credit   *Ev'ry bit of credit*
For it all belongs to you!   *For it all belongs to you!*

    [PICKERING *joins in this final musical bravo.*]

HIGGINS [*rising*]: All I can say is, thank God it's all over. Now I can go to bed at last without dreading tomorrow.

    [*The* SERVANTS *go off to bed.*]

MRS PEARCE: Good night, Mr Higgins. [*She, too, goes.*]

HIGGINS: Good night.

PICKERING: I think I shall turn in, too. It's been a great occasion. Good night, Higgins. [*He goes.*]

HIGGINS: Good night, Pickering. Oh, Mrs Pearce! [*But she is gone*] Oh damn, I meant to tell her I wanted coffee in the morning instead of tea. Leave a little note for her, Eliza, will you? [*He looks around the room*] What the devil have I done with my slippers?

    [*The slippers are by the desk.* ELIZA *tries to control herself, but no longer can. She hurls them at him with all her force.*]

ELIZA: There are your slippers! And there! Take your slippers, and may you never have a day's luck with them!

HIGGINS [*astounded*]: What on earth? [*He comes to her*] What's the matter? Is anything wrong?

ELIZA [*seething*]: Nothing wrong – with you. I've won your bet for you, haven't I? That's enough for you. I don't matter, I suppose?

HIGGINS: You won my bet! You! Presumptuous insect. *I* won it! What did you throw those slippers at me for?

ELIZA: Because I wanted to smash your face. I'd like to kill you, you selfish brute. Why didn't you leave me where you picked me out of – in the gutter? You thank God it's all over, and that now you can throw me back again there, do you?

HIGGINS [*looking at her in cool wonder*]: So the creature is nervous, after all?

[ELIZA *gives a suffocated scream of fury and instinctively darts her nails in his face.* HIGGINS *catches her wrists.*]

Ah! Claws in you, you cat! How dare you show your temper to me? [*He throws her roughly onto the sofa*] Sit down and be quiet.

ELIZA [*crushed by superior strength and weight*]: What's to become of me? What's to become of me?

HIGGINS: How the devil do I know what's to become of you? What does it matter what becomes of you?

ELIZA: You don't care. I know you don't care. You wouldn't care if I was dead. I'm nothing to you – not so much as them slippers.

HIGGINS [*thundering*]: *Those* slippers.

ELIZA [*with bitter submission*]: Those slippers. I didn't think it made any difference now.

[*A pause.* ELIZA *hopeless and crushed,* HIGGINS *a little uneasy.*]

HIGGINS [*in his loftiest manner*]: Why have you suddenly begun going on like this? May I ask whether you complain of your treatment here?

ELIZA: No.

HIGGINS: Has anybody behaved badly to you? Colonel Pickering? Mrs Pearce?

ELIZA: No.

HIGGINS: You don't pretend that I have treated you badly?

ELIZA: No.

HIGGINS: I'm glad to hear it. [*He moderates his tone*] Perhaps you're tired after the strain of the day? [*He picks up a box of chocolates*] Have a chocolate?

ELIZA: No. [*Recollecting her manners.*] Thank you.

HIGGINS [*good-humoured again*]: I suppose it was natural for you to be anxious, but it's all over now. [*He pats her kindly on the shoulder. She writhes.*] There's nothing more to worry about.

ELIZA: No, nothing more for you to worry about. Oh God, I wish I was dead.

HIGGINS [*in sincere surprise*]: Why, in Heaven's name, why? Listen to me, Eliza. All this irritation is purely subjective.

ELIZA: I don't understand. I'm too ignorant.

HIGGINS: It's only imagination. Nobody's hurting you. Nothing's wrong. You go to bed like a good girl, and sleep it off. Have a little cry and say your prayers; that will make you comfortable.

ELIZA: I heard your prayers. 'Thank God it's all over!'

HIGGINS [*impatiently*]: Well, don't you thank God it's all over? Now you are free and can do what you like.

ELIZA [*pulling herself together in desperation*]: What am I fit for? What have you left me fit for? Where am I to go? What am I to do? What's to become of me?

HIGGINS [*enlightened, but not at all impressed*]: Oh, that's what's worrying you, is it? [*Condescending to a trivial subject out of pure kindness*] Oh, I shouldn't bother about that if I were you. I should imagine you won't have much difficulty in settling yourself somewhere or other – though I hadn't quite realized you were going away. You might marry, you know. You see, Eliza, all men are not confirmed old bachelors like me and the Colonel. Most men are the marrying sort, poor devils. And you're not bad-looking. It's quite a pleasure to look at you at times. [*He looks at her*] Not now, of course. You've been crying and look like the very devil; but when you're all right and quite yourself, you're what I should call attractive. Come, you go to bed and have a good night's rest; and then get up and look at yourself in the glass; and you won't feel so cheap. [*Peering into the box of chocolates, in search of a creamy one. In the process, a genial after-thought occurs to him.*] I daresay my mother could find some chap or other who would do very well.

ELIZA: We were above that in Covent Garden.

HIGGINS: What do you mean?

ELIZA: I sold flowers. I didn't sell myself. Now you've made a lady of me, I'm not fit to sell anything else.

HIGGINS: Tosh, Eliza, don't insult human relations by dragging all that cant about buying and selling into it. [*Not finding a creamy one, he puts the chocolates down*] You needn't marry the fellow if you don't want to.

ELIZA: What else am I to do?

HIGGINS: Oh, lots of things. What about that old idea of a florist's shop? Pickering could set you up in one. He's lots of money. [*Chuckling*] He'll have to pay for all those togs you've been wearing; and that, with the hire of the jewelry, will make a big hole in two hundred pounds. Oh, come! You'll be all right. I must clear off to bed; I'm devilish sleepy. By the way, I was looking for something. What was it?

ELIZA: Your slippers.

HIGGINS: Yes, of course. You shied them at me.

[*He picks them up and is starting for the stairs when she rises and speaks to him.*]

ELIZA: Before you go, sir –

HIGGINS [*stopping, surprised at her calling him 'sir'*]: Eh?

ELIZA: Do my clothes belong to me or to Colonel Pickering?

HIGGINS [*coming back to her as if her question were the very climax of unreason*]: What the devil use would they be to Pickering? Why need you start bothering about that in the middle of the night?

ELIZA: I want to know what I may take away with me. I don't want to be accused of stealing.

HIGGINS [*deeply wounded*]: Stealing? You shouldn't have said that, Eliza. That shows a want of feeling.

ELIZA. I'm sorry. I'm only a common, ignorant girl; and in my station, I have to be careful. There can't be any feelings between the like of you and the like of me. Please will you tell me what belongs to me and what doesn't?

HIGGINS [*very sulky*]: You may take the whole damned houseful if you like. Except the jewels. They're hired. Will that satisfy you? [*He turns on his heels and is about to go in extreme dudgeon.*]

ELIZA [*drinking in his emotion like nectar and nagging him to provoke a further supply*]: Stop, please! [*She takes off her jewels*] Will you take these to your room and keep them safe? I don't want to run the risk of their being missing.

HIGGINS [*furious*]: Hand them over!

[*She gives him the jewels, he crams them into his pocket, unconsciously decorating himself with the protruding ends of the chains.*]

If these belonged to me instead of the jeweller, I'd ram them down your ungrateful throat.

ELIZA [*taking a ring off*]: This ring isn't the jeweller's; it's the one you bought me in Brighton. I don't want it now. [*He throws the ring violently across the room and turns on her so threateningly that she crouches with her hands over her face, and exclaims*] Don't you hit me.

HIGGINS: Hit you! You infamous creature, how dare you accuse me of such a thing? It is you who have hit me. You have wounded me to the heart.

ELIZA [*thrilling with hidden joy*]: I'm glad. I've got a little of my own back, anyhow.

HIGGINS [*with dignity, in his finest professional style*]: You have caused me to lose my temper, a thing that has hardly ever happened to me before. I prefer to say nothing more tonight. I am going to bed. [*He starts up the stairs.*]

ELIZA [*pertly*]: You'd better leave your own note for Mrs Pearce about the coffee, for it won't be done by me!

HIGGINS [*stopping about half-way up the stairs*]: Damn Mrs Pearce! And damn the coffee! And damn you! And damn my own folly in having lavished my hard-earned knowledge and the treasure of my regard and intimacy on a heartless gutter-snipe!

[*He marches up the stairs with impressive decorum and spoils it by tripping on the top step. He successfully recovers but while looking to see if she noticed his awkwardness, he runs into the table and inadvertently turns on the machine. Guttural vowel sounds come pouring through the speaker. He turns it off violently and with a slam of the door, disappears.*]

[ELIZA *runs to the ring on the floor and picks it up.*]

ELIZA:

[*With smouldering fury*]
  Just you wait, Henry Higgins, just you wait!
  You'll be sorry but your tears'll be too late!

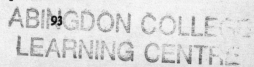

   You will be the one it's done to;
   And you'll have no one to run to;
   Just you wait, Henry Higgins, just you . . .
[She gives way to uncontrollable sobs.]

SCENE TWO

Outside HIGGINS' *house.*

Time: Immediately following.

At rise of curtain: FREDDY, *who has only left his post for changes of clothing, food, and sleep, is seated on the doorstep.*

FREDDY [*undaunted*]:

  Are there lilac trees in the heart of town?
  Can you hear a lark in any other part of town?
  Does enchantment pour
  Out of ev'ry door?
  No, it's just on the street where you live!

  And oh! the towering feeling
  Just to know somehow she is near!
  The overpowering feeling
  That any second you may suddenly appear!

  [ELIZA *comes out of the house. She is wearing a daytime suit and is carrying a small suitcase. For the moment,* FREDDY *doesn't see her.*]

People stop and stare. They don't . . .

  [*He sees her now*]

Darling!

ELIZA [*in a rage he does not understand*]: What are you doing here?

FREDDY: Nothing. I spend most of my time here. Oh, don't laugh at me, Miss Doolittle, but this is the only place . . .

ELIZA [*she puts down suitcase and grabs him by the shoulders*]: Freddy, you don't think I'm a heartless guttersnipe, do you?

FREDDY: Oh, no, darling. How could you imagine such a thing? You know how I feel. I've written you two and three times a day telling you. Sheets and sheets . . .

Speak and the world is full of singing,
And I'm winging
Higher than the birds.
[*In disgust, she turns away*]
Touch and my heart begins to crumble,
The heavens tumble,
Darling, and I'm . . .

ELIZA:

[*Turning on him violently*]
Words!
Words! Words! I'm sick of words!
I get words all day through;
First from him, now from you!
Is that all you blighters can do?
[FREDDY *is frightened*]
Don't talk of stars
Burning above;
If you're in love,
Show me!

Tell me no dreams
Filled with desire.
If you're on fire,
Show me!
[*He opens his arms to show her and she pushes him away*]
Here we are together in the middle of the night!
Don't talk of spring! Just hold me tight!
Anyone who's ever been in love'll tell you that
This is no time for a chat!

Haven't your lips
Longed for my touch?
Don't say how much,
Show me! Show me!

Don't talk of love lasting through time.
Make me no undying vow.
Show me now!

[*Bewildered but happy, he reaches for her again. She grabs his arm and fairly flings him down the street.*]

Sing me no song!
Read me no rhyme!
Don't waste my time,
Show me!

Don't talk of June!
Don't talk of fall!
Don't talk at all!
Show me!

Never do I ever want to hear another word.
There isn't one I haven't heard.
Here we are together in what ought to be a dream;
Say one more word and I'll scream!

Haven't your arms
Hungered for mine?
Please don't 'expl'ine'
Show me! Show me!

Don't wait until wrinkles and lines
Pop out all over my brow,
Show me now!

[*She picks up her suitcase and answers the longing look in his eyes by crowning him with it. Having released some of her anger against mankind in general, she marches off. He follows her, his arms out.*]

FREDDY: Darling ... Darling ...!

SCENE THREE

Covent Garden. The Flower Market. A huge glass-enclosed market centre.
There is a public house just outside.

Time: 5.00 that morning.

At rise of curtain: The market is coming to life. At first a few then
more and more vendors and flower girls walk on and prepare for business. A
few COSTERMONGERS *warm themselves around the smudge-pot fire. In*
the group are four who were warming themselves the night HIGGINS *first*
met ELIZA. *One of them starts whistling a few bars of the tune they sang.*
Three others pick it up.

MEN AT THE FIRE:

> *With one enormous chair . . .*
> *Oh wouldn't it be loverly?*
> *Lots of choc'late for me to eat;*
> *Lots of coal makin' lots of heat;*
> *Warm face, warm hands, warm feet . . .*
> *Oh, wouldn't it be loverly?*

[ELIZA *walks into view and gazes around. She sees two flower girls*
she used to know and goes over to them. They jump to their feet as if
they recognize her, then feel they've made a mistake and walk quickly
away, one of them remarking that this 'swell' looks very much like
ELIZA DOOLITTLE.]

[ELIZA *sees the men at the fire and hesitantly walks toward them*]

> *Oh, so loverly sittin' absobloominlutely still!*
> *I would never budge till spring*
> *Crept over me winder sill.*
> *Someone's head restin' on my knee;*
> *Warm and tender as he can be,*

    Who takes good care of me.
    Oh, wouldn't it be loverly . . .?
    Loverly! Loverly! . . .
[*They become aware of her presence, and their voices trail off. One of them rises.*]

THAT ONE: Good morning, miss. Can I help you?

ELIZA [*looking hopefully into his face*]: Do you mind if I warm my hands?

THAT ONE: Go right ahead, miss.
    [*She kneels down to warm her hands. They all stare at her uncomfortably. One of them leans forward as if he knows her.*]

ELIZA: Yes?

MAN LEANING FORWARD [*now leaning back*]: Excuse me, miss. For a second there I thought you was somebody else.

ELIZA: Who?

SAME MAN: Forgive me, ma'am. Early morning light playing tricks with me eyes.
    [*He rises. They all do.*]

FIRST MAN: Can I get you a taxi, ma'am? A lady like you shouldn't be walkin' around London at this hour of the mornin'.

ELIZA [*sadly*]: No . . . thank you.

SAME MAN: Good morning, miss.
    [*They all move away from her, somewhat embarrassed. Two of them keep looking back, feeling that they know her from somewhere.*]

ELIZA [*more alone than she has ever been, picks up a bunch of violets from a basket next to the fire and stares at it*]:
    Someone's head resting on my knee;
    Warm and tender as he can be,
    Who takes good care of me;
    Oh, wouldn't it be loverly . . .?
    Loverly! Loverly!
    Loverly! Loverly!
[*She is interrupted by a loud commotion from the pub.* HARRY *enters. He is quite well-dressed. He is followed by the* BARTENDER.]

HARRY: Well, goodnight to you, Cecil [*Calls into the pub*] Time to go, Alfie!

[DOOLITTLE *comes out of the pub. He is resplendently dressed as for a fashionable wedding and might be the bridegroom. A flower in his buttonhole, a dazzling silk hat, and patent leather shoes complete the effect.*]

BARTENDER: Do come again, Mr Doolittle. We value your patronage always.

DOOLITTLE [*grandly*]: Thank you, my good man. [*He gives him a generous tip*] Here, take the missus a trip to Brighton.

BARTENDER [*gratefully*]: Thank you, Mr Doolittle. [*He goes back into the pub.*]

ELIZA [*who has been watching, astounded*]: Father!

DOOLITTLE [*seeing her*]: You see, Harry, he has no mercy. Sent her down to spy on me in my misery, he did. Me own flesh and blood. [*He goes up to* ELIZA] Well, I'm miserable, all right. You can tell him that straight.

ELIZA: What are you talking about? What are you dressed up for?

DOOLITTLE: As if you didn't know! Go on back to that Wimpole Street devil and tell him what he done to me.

ELIZA: What has he done to you?

DOOLITTLE: He's ruined me, that's all. Destroyed me happiness. Tied me up and delivered me into the hands of middle-class morality. And don't you defend him. Was it him or was it not him that wrote to an old American blighter named Wallingford that was giving five millions to found moral reform societies, and tell him the most original moralist in England was Mr Alfred P. Doolittle, a common dustman?

ELIZA [*bitterly*]: That sounds like one of his jokes.

DOOLITTLE: You may call it a joke. It put the lid on me right enough! The bloke died and left me four thousand pounds a year in his bloomin' will.

JAMIE [*coming out of the pub*]: Oh, come on, Alfie. In a couple of hours you have to be at the church.

[*A group of* DOOLITTLE's *friends also emerge and motion him to come on back.*]

ELIZA: Church?

DOOLITTLE [*tragically*]: Yes, church. The deepest cut of all. Why do you think I'm dressed up like a ruddy pall-bearer? Your step-mother wants to marry me. Now I'm respectable – she wants to be respectable.

ELIZA: If that's the way you feel, why don't you give the money back?

DOOLITTLE [*with melancholy resignation*]: That's the tragedy of it, Eliza. It's easy to say chuck it, but I haven't the nerve. We're all intimidated. Intimidated, *Eliza*, that's what we are. And that's what I am. Bought up. That's what your precious professor has brought me to.

ELIZA: Not my precious professor.

DOOLITTLE: Oh, sent you back, has he? First he shoves me in the middle-class, then he chucks you out for me to support you. All part of his plan. [*Resourcefully*] But you doublecross him, Eliza. Don't you come home to me. Don't you take tuppence from me. You stand on your own two feet. You're a lady now and you can do it.

[FREDDY *appears through the crowd.*]

FREDDY: Eliza, it's getting awfully cold in that taxi.

DOOLITTLE: I say, you want to come and see me turned off this mornin'? St George's, Hanover Square, ten o'clock. [*Sadly*] I wouldn't advise it, but you're welcome.

ELIZA: No, thank you, Dad.

FREDDY [*to* ELIZA]: Are you all finished here?

ELIZA [*with great finality*]: Yes, Freddy. I'm all finished here. [*She takes his arm*] Good luck, Dad.

[*As a last gesture of farewell, she tosses away the violets and goes off with* FREDDY. DOOLITTLE *watches her go, rubbing his hands in satisfaction at having disposed of a knotty problem.*]

JAMIE: Come along, Alfie.

DOOLITTLE: How much time do I have left?

JAMIE, HARRY, AND FRIENDS:

> There's just a few more hours.
> That's all the time you've got.
> A few more hours
> Before they tie the knot.

[DOOLITTLE *bows his head in despair.*]

DOOLITTLE: There are drinks and girls all over London, and I have to track 'em down in just a few more hours.

> I'm getting married in the morning!
> Ding dong! the bells are gonna chime.
> Pull out the stopper!
> Let's have a whopper!
> But get me to the church on time!
>
> I gotta be there in the mornin'
> Spruced up and lookin' in me prime.
> Girls, come and kiss me;
> Show how you'll miss me.
> But get me to the church on time!
> If I am dancin'
> Roll up the floor.
> If I am whistlin'
> Whewt me out the door!
>
> For I'm gettin' married in the mornin'
> Ding dong! the bells are gonna chime.
> Kick up a rumpus
> But don't lose the compass;
> And get me to the church,
> Get me to the church,
> For Gawd's sake, get me to the church on time!

DOOLITTLE AND EVERYONE:

> I'm getting married in the morning
> Ding dong! the bells are gonna chime.

DOOLITTLE:

> *Drug me or jail me,*
> *Stamp me and mail me.*

ALL:

> *But get me to the church on time!*

> *I gotta be there in the morning*
> *Spruced up and lookin' in me prime.*

DOOLITTLE:

> *Some bloke who's able*
> *Lift up the table,*

ALL:

> *And get me to the church on time!*

DOOLITTLE:

> *If I am flying*
> *Then shoot me down.*
> *If I am wooin',*
> *Get her out of town!*

ALL:

> *For I'm getting married in the morning!*
> *Ding dong! the bells are gonna chime.*

DOOLITTLE:

> *Feather and tar me;*
> *Call out the Army;*
> *But get me to the church.*

ALL:

> *Get me to the church . . .*

DOOLITTLE:

> *For Gawd's sake, get me to the church on time!!*

[*The* CROWD *pulls out the stopper and has a whopper; a final street dance of farewell. When it's over, dawn begins to make her presence known through the glass roof.* DOOLITTLE's *friends line up to bid him a formal good-bye.*]

HARRY AND EVERYONE:

> *Starlight is reelin' home to bed now.*
> *Mornin' is smearin' up the sky.*
> *London is wakin'.*
> *Daylight is breakin'.*
> *Good luck, old chum,*
> *Good health, good-bye.*

DOOLITTLE:

> [*Solemnly shakes hands with all. In deepest gloom.*]
> *I'm gettin' married in the mornin'*
> *Ding dong! the bells are gonna chime ...*
> *Hail and salute me*
> *Then haul off and boot me ...*
> *And get me to the church,*
> *Get me to the church ...*
> *For Gawd's sake, get me to the church on time!*

> [DOOLITTLE *is lifted high in the air and carried off to the grim inevitable.*]

SCENE FOUR

The upstairs hall of HIGGINS' *house. There are three doors on the corridor and a telephone table and telephone.*

    Time: Around 11.00, *the following morning.*

    At rise of curtain: HIGGINS *is bellowing from his room.*

HIGGINS: Pickering! Pickering!

    [*He charges out of his room, followed by* MRS PEARCE. *Having not finished dressing, he is wearing a dressing gown. He knocks violently on* PICKERING's *door.*]

    Pickering! [*To* MRS PEARCE] Didn't she say where to send her clothes?

MRS PEARCE: I told you, sir, she took them all with her.

PICKERING [*entering, dressed*]: What? What?

HIGGINS: Here's a confounded thing! Eliza's bolted!

PICKERING: Bolted?

HIGGINS: Yes, bolted! And Mrs Pearce let her go without telling me a word about it.

PICKERING: Well, I'm dashed!

HIGGINS [*pacing distractedly up and down*]: What am I to do? I got tea this morning instead of coffee. I can't find anything. I don't know what appointments I've got.

MRS PEARCE: Eliza would know.

HIGGINS [*rage and frustration*]: Of course she would, but damn it, she's gone.

MRS PEARCE: Did either of you gentlemen frighten her last night?

PICKERING: You were there, Mrs Pearce. We hardly said a word to her. [*Turning on* HIGGINS] Higgins, did you bully her after I went to bed?

HIGGINS: Just the other way around. She threw the slippers at me. I never gave her the slightest provocation. The slippers came bang at my head before I uttered a word. And she used the most perfectly awful language. I was shocked.

PICKERING [*stunned*]: Well, I'm dashed.

HIGGINS: I don't understand it. She was shown every possible consideration. She admitted it herself.

PICKERING [*stunned*]: Well, I'm dashed.

HIGGINS [*wildly*]: For God's sake, Pickering, stop being dashed and do something.

PICKERING: What?

HIGGINS: Call the police! What are they there for, in Heaven's name? [*He starts into his room.*]

MRS PEARCE [*stopping him*]: Mr Higgins, you can't give Eliza's name to the police as if she were a thief, or a lost umbrella.

HIGGINS: Why not? I want to find her! The girl belongs to me! I paid five pounds for her! [*He charges into his room.*]

PICKERING: Quite right. [*He picks up phone*] Scotland Yard, please. May I have some coffee, Mrs Pearce?

MRS PEARCE: Yes, sir. [*She goes.*]

PICKERING [*sunnily, into phone*]: Oh, good morning, old chap. Colonel Hugh Pickering, here . . . 27a Wimpole Street. I want to report a missing person. Anything you can do to assist in her recovery will be frightfully appreciated. I'm not without influence, and I'll see to it that your superior. . . . Oh, yes. Eliza Doolittle . . . about twenty-one . . . I should say about five foot seven . . . Her eyes?

HIGGINS [*yelling from his room*]: Brown!

PICKERING [*into the phone*]: Brown . . . Her hair? Well, it's a rather neutral, nondescript colour. I should say more on the . . .

HIGGINS [*bounding from his room*]: Brown! Brown! Brown! [*Bounding back into his room.*]

PICKERING [*into the phone*]: Well, you heard what he said: brown . . .

Yes, this is her residence . . . Between three and four in the morning
. . . No . . . No . . . No . . . No relation at all. Let's just say a good
friend. [*He laughs good-humouredly*] Hmph? [*A troubled look clouds
his face*] Now, see here, my good man, I'm not at all pleased with
the tenor of that question. What the girl does here is our affair.
Your affair is to get her back so she can continue doing it! [*He hangs
up furious with the inspector.* HIGGINS *comes out of his room. He is now
almost dressed. Vexation knots his face.*]

HIGGINS:

> *What in all of Heaven could have prompted her to go?*
> *After such a triumph at the ball?*
> *What could have depressed her?*
> *What could have possessed her?*
> *I cannot understand the wretch at all!*

[*Shaking his head in exasperation, he goes back into his room to
finish dressing.*]

PICKERING [*who was only half listening, hits upon an idea. Calling to*
HIGGINS]: Higgins, I have an old school chum at the Home Office.
Perhaps he can help. I'll call him. [*Picks up phone*] Whitehall seven,
two, double four, please. [*He waits.*]

[HIGGINS *enters, struggling with his tie.*]

HIGGINS:

> *Women are irrational, that's all there is to that!*
> *Their heads are full of cotton, hay, and rags!*
> *They're nothing but exasperating, irritating,*
> *Vacillating, calculating, agitating,*
> *Maddening, and infuriating hags!*

[*He returns to his room.*]

PICKERING [*into the phone*]: Brewster Budgin, please . . . Yes, I'll
wait! [*He waits.*]

[HIGGINS *enters.*]

HIGGINS: Pickering, why can't a woman be more like a man?

> [PICKERING *looks at him, startled.*]
> *Yes. Why can't a woman be more like a man?*

Men are so honest, so thoroughly square;
Eternally noble, historically fair;
Who when you win will always give your back a pat.
Why can't a woman be like that?
Why does ev'ryone do what the others do?
Can't a woman learn to use her head?
Why do they do everything their mothers do?
Why don't they grow up like their fathers instead?
Why can't a woman take after a man?
Men are so pleasant, so easy to please;
Whenever you're with them, you're always at ease.
Would you be slighted if I didn't speak for hours?

PICKERING: Of course not.

HIGGINS:

Would you be livid if I had a drink or two?

PICKERING: Nonsense.

HIGGINS:

Would you be wounded if I never sent you flowers?

PICKERING: Never.

HIGGINS:

Why can't a woman be like you?
One man in a million may shout a bit.
Now and then there's one with slight defects.
One perhaps whose truthfulness you doubt a bit.
But by and large we are a marvellous sex!

Why can't a woman behave like a man?
Men are so friendly, good-natured, and kind;
A better companion you never will find.
If I were hours late for dinner, would you bellow?

PICKERING: Of course not.

HIGGINS:

If I forgot your silly birthday, would you fuss?

PICKERING: Nonsense.

HIGGINS:

Would you complain if I took out another fellow?

PICKERING: Never.

HIGGINS:

Why can't a woman be like us?

[*Livid that they're not, he goes back into his room slamming the door behind him.*]

PICKERING [*into phone*]: Hello, is Brewster Budgin there, please? [*Pause*] Boozy? You'll never, never, never guess who this is! [*Disappointed*] . . . Yes, it is. By George, what a memory! How are you, old fellow? It's so good to hear your voice again . . . Thirty years? It is really? Yes . . . oceans of water . . . yes . . . Boozy, old chap, I'll tell you why I called. Something rather unpleasant has happened at this end. Could I come right over and see you? Oh, good. I'll be right there. Thank you, Boozy. [*He hangs up as* MRS PEARCE *enters with the coffee*] I'm going over to the Home Office, Mrs Pearce.

MRS PEARCE: I do hope you find her, Colonel Pickering. Mr Higgins will miss her.

PICKERING: Mr Higgins will miss her! Blast Mr Higgins! I'll miss her! [*He goes.*]

[MRS PEARCE *places the coffee on the table as* HIGGINS *comes out of his room, now fully dressed.*]

HIGGINS: Pickering! Pickering! [*He looks around*] Where's the Colonel?

MRS PEARCE: He's gone to the Home Office, sir.

HIGGINS: Ah! You see, Mrs Pearce? I'm disturbed and he runs to help. [*Touched*] Now there's a good fellow. Mrs Pearce, you're a woman,

Why can't a woman be more like a man?
Men are so decent, such regular chaps.
Ready to help you through any mishaps.
Ready to buck you up whenever you are glum.
Why can't a woman be a chum?

Why is thinking something women never do?
Why is logic never ever tried?
Straightening up their hair is all they ever do.
Why don't they straighten up the mess that's inside?

Why can't a woman be more like a man?
If I were a woman who'd been to a ball,
Been hailed as a princess by one and by all;
Would I start weeping like a bathtub overflowing?
And carry on as if my home were in a tree?
Would I run off and never tell me where I'm going?
Why can't a woman be like me?
[*He clamps his hat on his head and stalks off.*]

SCENE FIVE

The conservatory of MRS HIGGINS' *house.*
  Time: Shortly after.
  At rise of curtain: MRS HIGGINS *and* ELIZA *are having tea.*

MRS HIGGINS: And you mean to say that after you did this wonderful thing for them without making a single mistake, they just sat there and never said a word to you? Never petted you, or admired you, or told you how splendid you'd been?

ELIZA: Not a word.

MRS HIGGINS: That's simply appalling. I should not have thrown the slippers at him, I should have thrown the fire irons.

  [ELIZA *smiles, but the smile is short-lived as* HIGGINS *is heard thundering from the entrance hall.*]

HIGGINS [*off*]: Mother! Mother!

  [ELIZA *looks fearful and rises to leave.*]

MRS HIGGINS [*staying her*]: I thought it wouldn't be long. Stay where you are, my dear.

HIGGINS [*off*]: Mother, where the devil are you?

MRS HIGGINS: Remember, last night you not only danced with a prince, but you behaved like a princess.

  [ELIZA *collects herself as* HIGGINS *charges into the room.*]

HIGGINS: Mother, the damndest ...! [*He sees* ELIZA. *Amazed. Angry.*] You!

ELIZA [*giving a staggering exhibition of ease of manner*]: How do you do, Professor Higgins? Are you quite well?

HIGGINS [*choking*]: Am I ... [*He can say no more.*]

ELIZA: But of course you are. You are never ill. Would you care for some tea?

HIGGINS: Don't you dare try that game on me! I taught it to you! Get up and come home and don't be a fool! You've caused me enough trouble for one morning!

MRS HIGGINS: Very nicely put, indeed, Henry. No woman could resist such an invitation.

HIGGINS: How did this baggage get here in the first place?

MRS HIGGINS: Eliza came to see me, and I was delighted to have her. And if you don't promise to behave yourself, I shall have to ask you to leave.

HIGGINS: You mean I'm to put on my Sunday manners for this thing I created out of the squashed cabbage leaves of Covent Garden?

MRS HIGGINS [*calmly*]: Yes, dear, that is precisely what I mean.

HIGGINS: I'll see her damned first! [*He walks to the rear of the conservatory and paces back and forth noisily.*]

MRS HIGGINS [*to* ELIZA]: How did you ever learn manners with my son around?

ELIZA [*sweetly, but making certain her voice carries*]: It was very difficult. I should never have known how ladies and gentlemen behave if it hadn't been for Colonel Pickering. He always showed me that he felt and thought about me as if I were something better than a common flower girl. You see, Mrs Higgins, apart from the things one can pick up, the difference between a lady and a flower girl is not how she behaves, but how she is treated. I shall always be a flower girl to Professor Higgins because he always treats me as a flower girl and always will. But I know that I shall always be a lady to Colonel Pickering because he always treats me as a lady, and always will.

[*There is a strange gnashing noise from the rear of the conservatory.*]

MRS HIGGINS: Henry, please don't grind your teeth.

[*The* PARLOUR-MAID *enters.*]

MAID: The vicar is here, madam. Shall I show him into the garden?

MRS HIGGINS [*horrified*]: The Vicar, and the Professor? Good Heavens, no! I'll see him in the library.

[*The* MAID *goes.* MRS HIGGINS *rises to follow.*]

Eliza, if my son begins to break things, I give you full permission to have him evicted. [*At the door, she turns back to* HIGGINS] Henry, dear, if I were you, I should stick to two subjects, the weather and your health. [*She goes.*]

[HIGGINS *comes down to the tea-table. He looks at* ELIZA *quizzically; while deciding on a method of attack he pours himself some tea. He decides on restraint.*]

HIGGINS: Well, Eliza, you've had a bit of your own back, as you call it. Have you had enough? And are you going to be reasonable? Or do you want any more?

ELIZA: You want me back only to pick up your slippers and put up with your tempers and fetch and carry for you.

HIGGINS: I haven't said I wanted you back at all.

ELIZA [*turns to him*]: Oh, indeed. Then what are we talking about?

HIGGINS: About you, not about me. If you come back I shall treat you just as I have always treated you. I can't change my nature; and I don't intend to change my manners. My manners are exactly the same as Colonel Pickering's.

ELIZA: That's not true. He treats a flower girl as if she was a duchess.

HIGGINS: And I treat a duchess as if she was a flower girl.

ELIZA: Oh, I see. [*She rises composedly and walks away*] The same to everybody.

HIGGINS: Just so. [*He sits at the table*] ... The great secret, Eliza, is not having bad manners or good manners or any other particular sort of manners, but having the same manner for all human souls. The question is not whether I treat you rudely, but whether you ever heard me treat anyone else better.

ELIZA [*with sudden sincerity*]: I don't care how you treat me. I don't mind you swearing at me. I shouldn't mind a black eye: I've had one before this. But I won't be passed over.

HIGGINS: Then get out of my way: for I won't stop for you. You talk about me as if I were a motor bus.

ELIZA: So you are a motor bus: all bounce and go, and no consideration for anyone. But I can get along without you. Don't think
I can't.

HIGGINS: I know you can. I told you you could. [*Pause, seriously*]
You never wondered, I suppose, whether I could get along without
you.

ELIZA: Don't try to get around me. You'll have to.

HIGGINS [*arrogantly*]: And so I can. Without you or any soul on
earth. [*With sudden humility*] But I shall miss you, Eliza. I've learned
something from your idiotic notions. I confess that humbly and
gratefully.

ELIZA: Well, you have my voice on your gramophone. When you
feel lonely without me you can turn it on. It's got no feelings to
hurt.

HIGGINS: I can't turn your soul on.

ELIZA: Oh, you are a devil. You can twist the heart in a girl as easily
as some can twist her arms to hurt her. What am I to come back for?

HIGGINS [*heartily*]: For the fun of it. That's why I took you on.

ELIZA: And you may throw me out tomorrow if I don't do everything you want me to?

HIGGINS: Yes: and you may walk out tomorrow if I don't do everything you want me to.

ELIZA: And live with my father?

HIGGINS: Yes, or sell flowers. Or would you rather marry Pickering?

ELIZA [*fiercely*]: I wouldn't marry you if you asked me; and you're
nearer my age than what he is.

HIGGINS [*correcting her gently*]: Than he is.

ELIZA [*losing her temper and walking away from him*]: I'll talk as I like.
You're not my teacher now. That's not what I want and don't
you think it. I've always had chaps enough wanting me that way.
Freddy Hill writes to me twice and three times a day, sheets and
sheets.

HIGGINS [*coming to her*]: Oh, in short, you want me to be as infatuated
about you as he is. Is that it?

ELIZA [*facing him, much troubled*]: No, I don't. That's not the sort of feeling I want from you. I want a little kindness. I know I'm a common ignorant girl, and you a book-learned gentleman; but I'm not dirt under your feet. What I done – [*Correcting herself*] What I did was not for the dresses and the taxis: I did it because we were pleasant together and I come – came to care for you; not to want you to make love to me, and not forgetting the difference between us, but more friendly like.

HIGGINS: Yes, of course. That's just how I feel. And how Pickering feels. Eliza, you're a fool.

ELIZA: That's not a proper answer to give me.

HIGGINS: It's all you'll get until you stop being a plain idiot. If you're going to be a lady you'll have to stop feeling neglected if the men you know don't spend half their time snivelling over you and the other half giving you black eyes. You find me cold, unfeeling, selfish, don't you? Very well: Be off with you to the sort of people you like. Marry some sentimental hog or other with lots of money, and a thick pair of lips to kiss you with and a thick pair of boots to kick you with. If you can't appreciate what you've got, you'd better get what you can appreciate.

ELIZA [*desperate*]: I can't talk to you: you turn everything against me. I'm always in the wrong. But don't you be too sure that you have me under your feet to be trampled on and talked down. I'll marry Freddy, I will, as soon as I'm able to support him.

HIGGINS [*disagreeably surprised*]: Freddy!! That poor devil who couldn't get a job as an errand boy even if he had the guts to try for it! Woman, do you not understand? I have made you a consort for a king!

ELIZA: Freddy loves me: that makes him king enough for me. I don't want him to work: he wasn't brought up to it as I was. [*Determinedly*] I'll go and be a teacher.

HIGGINS: What'll you teach, in heaven's name?

ELIZA: What you taught me. I'll teach phonetics.

HIGGINS: Ha! Ha! Ha!

ELIZA: I'll offer myself as an assistant to that brilliant Hungarian!

HIGGINS [*in a fury*]: What! That impostor! That humbug! That toadying ignoramus! Teach him my methods! My discoveries? [*He strides towards her*] You take one step in that direction and I'll wring your neck. Do you hear?

ELIZA [*defiantly non-resistant*]: Wring away! What do I care? I knew you'd strike me one day. [HIGGINS, *about to lay hands on her, recoils*] Aha! That's done you, 'enry 'iggins, it 'as. Now I don't care that – [*she snaps her fingers in his face*] for your bullying and your big talk.

> *What a fool I was! What a dominated fool!*
> *To think you were the earth and sky.*
> *What a fool I was! What an addle-pated fool!*
> *What a mutton-headed dolt was I!*
> *No, my reverberating friend,*
> *You are not the beginning and the end!*

HIGGINS [*wondering at her*]: You impudent hussy! There isn't an idea in your head or a word in your mouth that I haven't put there!

ELIZA:

> *There'll be spring ev'ry year without you.*
> *England still will be here without you.*
> *There'll be fruit on the tree,*
> *And a shore by the sea;*
> *There'll be crumpets and tea*
> *Without you.*
>
> *Art and music will thrive without you.*
> *Somehow Keats will survive without you.*
> *And there still will be rain*
> *On that plain down in Spain,*
> *Even that will remain*
> *Without you.*
> *I can do*
> *Without you.*

> *You, dear friend, who talk so well,*
> *You can go to Hertford, Hereford, and Hampshire!*
> *They can still rule the land without you.*
> *Windsor Castle will stand without you.*
> *And without much ado*
> *We can all muddle through*
> *Without you!*

HIGGINS [*fascinated*]: You brazen hussy!

ELIZA:

> *Without your pulling it, the tide comes in,*
> *Without your twirling it, the earth can spin.*
> *Without your pushing them, the clouds roll by.*
> *If they can do without you, ducky, so can I!*

> *I shall not feel alone without you.*
> *I can stand on my own without you.*
> *So go back in your shell,*
> *I can do bloody well*
> *Without ...*

HIGGINS [*triumphantly*]:

> *By George, I really did it!*
> *I did it! I did it!*
> *I said I'd make a woman*
> *And indeed I did!*

> *I knew that I could do it!*
> *I knew it! I knew it!*
> *I said I'd make a woman*
> *And succeed I did!*

Eliza, you're magnificent! Five minutes ago you were a millstone around my neck. Now you're a tower of strength, a consort battleship! I like you like this!

[ELIZA *stares at him stonily, then turns on her heels and walks to the door.*]

ELIZA [*quietly at the door*]: Good-bye, Professor Higgins. I shall not be seeing you again. [*She goes.*]

[HIGGINS *is thunderstruck. He walks falteringly across the room and looks after her.*]

HIGGINS [*calling for help*]: Mother! Mother!

[MRS HIGGINS *enters.*]

MRS HIGGINS: What is it, Henry? What has happened?

HIGGINS [*more to himself*]: She's gone!

MRS HIGGINS [*gently*]: Of course, dear. What did you expect?

HIGGINS [*bewildered*]: What am I to do?

MRS HIGGINS: Do without, I suppose.

HIGGINS [*with sudden defiance*]: And so I shall! If the Higgins oxygen burns up her little lungs, let her seek some stuffiness that suits her. She's an owl sickened by a few days of my sunshine! Very well, let her go! I can do without her! I can do without anybody! I have my own soul! My own spark of divine fire! [*He marches off.*]

MRS HIGGINS [*applauding*]: Bravo, Eliza! [*She smiles.*]

SCENE SIX

Outside HIGGINS' *house, Wimpole Street.*
Time: Dusk, that afternoon.
At rise of curtain: HIGGINS *enters bellowing with rage.*

HIGGINS: Damn!! Damn!! Damn!! Damn!! [*A sudden terrifying discovery*] I've grown accustomed to her face!

> *She almost makes the day begin.*
> *I've grown accustomed to the tune*
> *She whistles night and noon.*
> *Her smiles. Her frowns.*
> *Her ups, her downs,*
> *Are second nature to me now;*
> *Like breathing out and breathing in.*
> [*Reassuringly.*]
> *I was serenely independent and content before we met;*
> *Surely I could always be that way again –*
> [*The reassurance fails.*]
>   *and yet*
>
> *I've grown accustomed to her looks;*
> *Accustomed to her voice:*
> *Accustomed to her face.*

[*Bitterly*] Marry Freddy! What an infantile idea! What a heartless, wicked, brainless thing to do! But she'll regret it! She'll regret it! It's doomed before they even take the vow!

> *I can see her now:*
> *Mrs Freddy Eynsford-Hill,*
> *In a wretched little flat above a store.*

I can see her now:
Not a penny in the till,
And a bill-collector beating at the door.

She'll try to teach the things I taught her,
And end up selling flow'rs instead;
Begging for her bread and water,
While her husband has his breakfast in bed!
[Fiendishly pleased]
In a year or so
When she's prematurely grey,
And the blossom in her cheek has turned to chalk,
She'll come home and lo!
He'll have upped and run away
With a social climbing heiress from New York!
[Tragically]
Poor Eliza!
How simply frightful!
How humiliating!
[Irresistibly]
How delightful!
[He walks to his door]

How poignant it will be on that inevitable night when she hammers on my door in tears and rags. Miserable and lonely, repentant and contrite. Will I let her in or hurl her to the wolves? Give her kindness, or the treatment she deserves? Will I take her back, or throw the baggage out?

[With sudden benevolence]
I'm a most forgiving man;
The sort who never could,
Ever would,
Take a position and staunchly never budge.
Just a most forgiving man.
[With sudden vindictiveness]

But I will never take her back,
If she were crawling on her knees.
Let her promise to atone!
Let her shiver, let her moan!
I will slam the door and let the hell-cat freeze!

Marry Freddy! Ha! [he takes out his keys to open the door but stops in despair]

But I'm so used to hear her say
Good morning every day.
Her joys, her woes,
Her highs, her lows
Are second nature to me now;
Like breathing out and breathing in.
I'm very grateful she's a woman
And so easy to forget;
Rather like a habit
One can always break – and yet
I've grown accustomed to the trace
Of something in the air;
Accustomed to her face.

SCENE SEVEN

HIGGINS' *study.*

Time: Immediately following.

At rise of curtain: The blue-grey light of early evening pours in through the window. Only one or two lamps are on.

HIGGINS *walks into the room. He walks around thoughtfully. He comes to the xylophone and picks up the mallet and looks at it for a moment. He slowly walks over to the machine by the door and turns it on.* ELIZA's *voice is heard on the speaker. He goes back to his desk and decides to sit on the stool rather than his own chair behind the desk. His hat still on, his head bowed, he listens to the recording.*

ELIZA's VOICE: I want to be a lady in a flower shop instead of selling flowers at the corner of Tottenham Court Road. But they won't take me unless I talk more genteel. He said he could teach me. Well, here I am ready to pay, not asking any favour – and he treats me as if I was dirt. I know what lessons cost, and I'm ready to pay.

    [ELIZA *walks softly into the room and stands for a moment by the machine looking at* HIGGINS.]

HIGGINS' VOICE: It's almost irresistible. She's so deliciously low, so horribly dirty. [ELIZA *turns off the machine.*]

ELIZA [*gently*]: I washed my face and hands before I come, I did.

    [HIGGINS *straightens up. If he could but let himself, his face would radiate unmistakable relief and joy. If he could but let himself, he would run to her. Instead, he leans back with a contented sigh pushing his hat forward till it almost covers his face.*]

HIGGINS [*softly*]: Eliza? Where the devil are my slippers?

    [*There are tears in* ELIZA's *eyes. She understands.*]

        The curtain falls slowly.

READ MORE IN PENGUIN

In every corner of the world, on every subject under the sun, Penguin represents quality and variety – the very best in publishing today.

For complete information about books available from Penguin – including Puffins, Penguin Classics and Arkana – and how to order them, write to us at the appropriate address below. Please note that for copyright reasons the selection of books varies from country to country.

In the United Kingdom: Please write to *Dept. EP, Penguin Books Ltd, Bath Road, Harmondsworth, West Drayton, Middlesex UB7 0DA*

In the United States: Please write to *Consumer Sales, Penguin USA, P.O. Box 999, Dept. 17109, Bergenfield, New Jersey 07621-0120*. VISA and MasterCard holders call 1-800-253-6476 to order Penguin titles

In Canada: Please write to *Penguin Books Canada Ltd, 10 Alcorn Avenue, Suite 300, Toronto, Ontario M4V 3B2*

In Australia: Please write to *Penguin Books Australia Ltd, P.O. Box 257, Ringwood, Victoria 3134*

In New Zealand: Please write to *Penguin Books (NZ) Ltd, Private Bag 102902, North Shore Mail Centre, Auckland 10*

In India: Please write to *Penguin Books India Pvt Ltd, 706 Eros Apartments, 56 Nehru Place, New Delhi 110 019*

In the Netherlands: Please write to *Penguin Books Netherlands bv, Postbus 3507, NL-1001 AH Amsterdam*

In Germany: Please write to *Penguin Books Deutschland GmbH, Metzlerstrasse 26, 60594 Frankfurt am Main*

In Spain: Please write to *Penguin Books S. A., Bravo Murillo 19, 1° B, 28015 Madrid*

In Italy: Please write to *Penguin Italia s.r.l., Via Felice Casati 20, I–20124 Milano*

In France: Please write to *Penguin France S. A., 17 rue Lejeune, F–31000 Toulouse*

In Japan: Please write to *Penguin Books Japan, Ishikiribashi Building, 2–5–4, Suido, Bunkyo-ku, Tokyo 112*

In South Africa: Please write to *Longman Penguin Southern Africa (Pty) Ltd, Private Bag X08, Bertsham 2013*

READ MORE IN PENGUIN

A CHOICE OF FICTION

The Year at Thrush Green Miss Read

Winter at Thrush Green flows into a beautiful spring and a series of local dramas takes hold of the village community. Plans for the village fête are hotting up, problems concerning the Rectory Cottages prove difficult to solve and the arrival of a stranger from America excites much interest . . .

Lucia Victrix E. F. Benson

Outrageously funny and wickedly satirical, E. F. Benson's portrait of society in the glamorous 1920s is as endlessly entertaining today as when it was first published.

Travels with My Aunt Graham Greene

In *Travels with My Aunt* Graham Greene not only gives us intoxicating entertainment but also confronts us with some of the most perplexing of human dilemmas.

The Folks That Live on the Hill Kingsley Amis

'In this utterly entertaining piece, Kingsley Amis proves once more that no one can hold a candle to his blistering command of contemporary life – and letters' – *Mail on Sunday*

Heavy Weather P. G. Wodehouse

Lord Tilbury, the Napoleon of Fleet Street, is not feeling his usual self. The Hon. Galahad Threepwood's sudden refusal to have his scurrilous memoirs published will be a grave financial loss to Tilbury and he hopes to pursuade him otherwise. Enter Monty Bodkin . . .

The World of Mrs Harris Paul Gallico

The complete adventures of Ada Harris (pronounced 'Arris), spirited, game-for-anything charlady of Willis Road, Battersea. Carrying with her a magical ability to put things right, a sympathetic twinkle in her eye and an unswerving faith in 'Im Above, Mrs Harris is one of Paul Gallico's most delightful and uplifting characters.

READ MORE IN PENGUIN

A CHOICE OF FICTION

Felicia's Journey William Trevor
Winner of the 1994 Whitbread Book of the Year Award

Vividly and with heart-aching insight William Trevor traces the desperate
plight of a young Irish girl scouring the post-industrial Midlands for her
lover. Unable to find Johnny, she is, instead, found by Mr Hilditch, pudgy
canteen manager, collecter and befriender of homeless young girls.

The Eye in the Door Pat Barker

'Barker weaves fact and fiction to spellbinding effect, conjuring up the
vastness of the First World War through its chilling impact on the minds
of the men who endured it . . . a startlingly original work of fiction . . . it
extends the boundaries not only of the anti-war novel, but of fiction
generally' – *Sunday Telegraph*

The Heart of It Barry Hines

Cal Rickards, a successful scriptwriter, is forced to return to the Yorkshire
mining town of his youth when his father, a leading voice in the 1980s
miners' strike, suddenly becomes ill. Gradually, as Cal delves into his
family's past and faces unsettling memories, he comes to reassess his own
future.

Dr Haggard's Disease Patrick McGrath

'The reader is compellingly drawn into Dr Haggard's life as it begins to
unfold through episodic flashbacks . . . It is a beautiful story, impressively
told, with a restraint and a grasp of technicality that command belief, and
a lyricism that gives the description of the love affair the sort of epic
quality rarely found these days' – *The Times*

A Place I've Never Been David Leavitt

'Wise, witty and cunningly fuelled by narrative . . . another high calibre
collection by an unnervingly mature young writer' – *Sunday Times*.
'Leavitt can make a world at a stroke and people it with convincing
characters . . . humane, touching and beautifully written' – *Observer*

READ MORE IN PENGUIN

A SELECTION OF PLAYS

Edward Albee	**Who's Afraid of Virginia Woolf?**
	Three Tall Women
Alan Ayckbourn	**Joking Apart and Other Plays**
James Baldwin	**The Amen Corner**
Dermot Bolger	**A Dublin Quartet**
Bertolt Brecht	**Parables for the Theatre**
Albert Camus	**Caligula and Other Plays**
Anton Chekhov	**Plays (The Cherry Orchard/Three Sisters/ Ivanov/The Seagull/Uncle Vanya)**
Brian Friel	**Molly Sweeney**
Henrik Ibsen	**A Doll's House/League of Youth/Lady from the Sea**
Eugène Ionesco	**Rhinoceros/The Chairs/The Lesson**
Ben Jonson	**Three Comedies (Volpone/The Alchemist/ Bartholomew Fair)**
D. H. Lawrence	**Three Plays (The Collier's Friday Night/ The Daughter-in-Law/The Widowing of Mrs Holroyd)**
Mike Leigh	**Abigail's Party/Goose-Pimples**
Arthur Miller	**Death of a Salesman**
Peter Shaffer	**The Royal Hunt of the Sun**
	Equus
Bernard Shaw	**Plays Pleasant**
	Pygmalion
	John Bull's Other Island
Sophocles	**Three Theban Plays (Oedipus the King/ Antigone/Oedipus at Colonus)**
Keith Waterhouse	**Jeffrey Bernard is Unwell and Other Plays**
Arnold Wesker	**Plays, Volumes 1-7**
Oscar Wilde	**The Importance of Being Earnest and Other Plays**
Thornton Wilder	**Our Town/The Skin of Our Teeth/The Matchmaker**
Tennessee Williams	**Cat on a Hot Tin Roof/The Milk Train Doesn't Stop Here Anymore/The Night of the Iguana**